ILLIBERAL EUROPE

EASTERN EUROPE FROM THE FALL OF THE BERLIN WALL TO THE WAR IN UKRAINE

LEON MARC

OLDCASTLE BOOKS

OLDCASTLE BOOKS
This new edition first published in 2023 by
Oldcastle Books, Harpenden, Herts, UK
oldcastlebooks.com
@OldcastleBooks

Contains material originally published as
What's So Eastern About Eastern Europe? in 2009.

The views expressed in this book are the author's and do not necessarily
express the views of the organisation where he is employed.

Editor: Nick Rennison

A CIP catalogue record for this book is available from the British Library.

ISBN
978-0-85730-551-0 (Paperback)
978-0-85730-555-8 (eBook)

2 4 6 8 10 9 7 5 3 1

Typeset in 11.35 on 14.35pt Times New Roman
by Avocet Typeset, Bideford, Devon, EX39 2BP
Printed and bound by CPI Group (UK) Ltd, Croydon, CR0 4YY

CONTENTS

Prologue:
The Three Classmates

In late July 2003, I stood in a funeral home near Cobham in Surrey, paying my last respects to a man called Karl Lavrenčič. As the coffin was quietly sliding into the mouth of the crematorium, I was overwhelmed by my emotions. In this English suburb the slightly insecure voices of an amateur male group, singing traditional Slovenian funeral hymns, were something from another world. Watching his family and friends, and the Slovenian Catholic priest from London who was conducting the service, the thought slipped through my mind that this man died in the wrong place. Despite all that Karl did for his native country, it was his dying in England – the country that had long ago become his new and (most probably) truest home – that really gave the impression that he had been finally and forever lost to his fatherland.

Karl Lavrenčič, dubbed 'adventurous World Service broadcaster',[1] and his wife Dora were very good to me. I do not recall exactly how I first met him. It must have been on one of his trips to Slovenia. Formally retired, he continued his freelance work for the Economist Intelligence Unit, for the

---

1. https://www.independent.co.uk/news/obituaries/karl-lavrencic-36832.html (Retrieved on 23 June 2022.)

Slovenian Section of the BBC and for other organisations. His work meant everything to him.

Every morning, there were papers from all over the world waiting on the doorstep of his home in Oxshott. And despite his age – he was over 70 at the time – he still used to travel around the globe. Annual IMF and World Bank gatherings in Washington were his staple food, as were monthly trips to Slovenia. There, he walked into my office one day at one of the newly-emerged political parties, where I was in charge of international affairs. From then on, we kept in touch, and I was a welcome visitor to his and Dora's home. During my studies at the University of London, I often spent weeks there preparing for the exams.

He and Dora lived a very comfortable life by the time they both retired. But it was not always like that. Karl came to the UK with little more than the clothes he stood up in. Dora, the daughter of a senior Slovenian politician from the years before World War II, did not fare much better. She came from a respected conservative family of Slovenian patriots; he was the son of a liberal father, a former Austrian imperial teacher, and an ethnic-German mother. He managed to survive World War II but he was unhappy about the kind of liberty that Yugoslav Communists were able to deliver and, after a brief spell in prison, he fled the country. With his gift for languages he made his way through the displaced persons' camp in Austria to the UK. There he went through a number of jobs before he managed to settle at the BBC Slovenian service, finished a degree in economics (to add to the one in law he brought with him from home), and began what was to be a remarkable career in journalism. He toured the Communist world (described in *Living with Communism*, published in 1966 under the pseudonym of Anthony Silvester), but then he dedicated himself to Africa, which he knew inside out. Yet he never lost interest in Yugoslavia and Slovenia.

Karl was a law student, with a great interest in economics and international affairs, when World War II started. Two of his classmates at Ljubljana University at the time were men whose lives would continue to be intertwined with his in the future – Ljubo Sirc, the son of a wealthy businessman, and Aleksander Bajt, a former altar boy. Ljubo too ended up in the UK soon after the war, where he worked his way up to become a university professor in Glasgow. Another liberal but also a Yugoslav patriot, he was at first a firm believer in the idea of Tito's resistance movement which he joined. Yet this did not spare his father a death sentence, following a notorious show trial soon after the Communists came to power, and he himself narrowly escaped the same fate. Years later, he established in London the Centre for Research into Communist Economies, an academic think-tank researching the Communist economic experiment at a time when many Western academics seriously thought that it had something to offer. Ljubo wanted to warn them that this was not true.

Aleksander Bajt followed a different path. He came from a deeply religious family. So Karl was enormously surprised when, one morning after the war, he bumped into Aleksander, wearing the *partisan* uniform with the red star on his hat, and speaking passionately about the new world order that was being established in the country. According to Karl's later accounts, this meeting finally convinced Karl to leave the new Yugoslavia. Or, as he put it in his book, he left because he was 'unable to enjoy life in a closely regimented society'.

But Aleksander's story does not end there. He too had a great interest in economics. In fact, his red star helped him to make a career that he had probably never even dreamed about.

He was even able to found and run a relatively autonomous economics institute in Ljubljana, the Slovenian capital. As the Yugoslav and, in particular, the Slovenian socialist economy was flirting with the logic of capitalist economy, his institute grew in fame.

But his most nonconformist act came much later: his book, *Berman's Dossier* (written in Slovenian), was a bulky volume of a thousand-plus pages which few read in its entirety and it was completed almost literally on his deathbed. It shook many in Slovenia. By then, books critical of the Communist system were not that rare anymore. But it was shocking that Bajt, a respected scientist and a former partisan comrade himself, should present an utterly revisionist and devastatingly critical account of the partisan resistance and the Communist revolutionary movement.

Ljubo too got involved. With his eternal, almost naïve belief in the intrinsic good of mankind, he accepted after the democratic changes the challenge offered by a new political party (born out of the Socialist Youth Organisation that rebranded itself as the Liberal Democratic Party) and unsuccessfully ran for President of Slovenia, only to later feel that he had been used as a figurehead by men who did not exactly share his passionate and deep belief in liberal democracy. This word will feature prominently in the second part of this book.

Each of the three classmates could tell his own personal story about Eastern Europe as they knew it and each of these stories is so characteristic of Central and Eastern Europe to which this book is dedicated. Throughout it, the three terms (Central Europe, Eastern Europe and Central and Eastern Europe) will often be used interchangeably, as they often are in the English-speaking world, though I will also explain the distinctive nature of different parts of what is commonly known as Eastern Europe. This is also the main subject of the first part of the book.

Today, the Berlin Wall has been down for some time and the countries of the region safely in the European Union and NATO. Over the period of 30 years, knowledge about the region, including popular knowledge, has improved considerably. But the rise of Mr Kaczyński in Poland and Mr Orbán in Hungary and the region's reaction to the migrant crisis in 2015 have once again raised questions about the meaning of what is called Eastern Europe. The war in Ukraine has further revived interest in this part of the Continent.

Much of what is contained in the following pages was published in 2009 under the title *What's So Eastern About Eastern Europe?* The aim of the book then was to familiarise the reader with basic political and social history of the region. A lot of that has, as I said, now became a part of general knowledge and does not need to be repeated. But since then there have also been new developments that have puzzled Western audiences again and posed, albeit in a different way, the same question again: what is so different, after all, about Eastern Europe that, after successfully becoming a part of Europe again, it seems to have turned into what has become known as 'Illiberal Europe'? This is, at least, how it looks. This question calls for a new, revised and updated edition that retains most of the historical account of the first edition, but omits some of the now less relevant facts, and rather focuses on those aspects that put the so-called illiberal drift or democratic backslide into contemporary perspective.

The book concludes with a final chapter (and an epilogue) explaining the nature of and reasons for this backlash, and putting it into the context of the crisis of liberal democracy, as experienced in the global West today. And it is in this crisis too that – while certainly possessing its own specific problems – Central Europe remains very much a part of Europe and the global West, including when it comes to the current culture wars in the West. In fact, while this book is essentially about Eastern Europe, its political and cultural history, before and after the fall of the Berlin Wall, it also shows that the current challenges to the liberal order in this part of Europe are to a great extent an offshoot of the same trends in the West – and of its insecurity about itself in a dangerous time. What we are witnessing is not only about the choice between liberal and illiberal, but also between different interpretations of a liberal order. In this analysis of illiberal Europe, as well as in the search for a genuine and noble Western liberalism and a true and distinct European identity, Eastern Europe is therefore only a convenient geographic point of departure. More than just a question of geography, illiberal Europe is a state of mind worthy of exploration.

Introduction:
Eastern Europeans Descend on the West

Ruairi seemed rather lonely. In the Superquinn supermarket, in a wealthy Dublin suburb on a Saturday morning in the spring of 2005, he was one of the few Irish staff at the checkout. The girl serving us was from Lithuania, and my wife and I were also from what is described as Eastern Europe. The night before, we had had dinner in a Lebanese restaurant with a Slovakian couple. The two waitresses were Polish and the belly dancer was German, presumably former East German.

Within a couple of years since May 2004, the day of the EU accession of eight new Central European (and two southern European) member states, several hundred thousands of workers from these countries came to seek work in Ireland. The decision of the Irish government to end the system of work-permits for workers from new member states was hailed by the opposition, business and trade unions alike as a way of securing much needed extra labour for what was then called the Celtic Tiger. That was, of course, before the global financial crisis of 2007.

Apart from Ireland, only the UK opened its labour market equally generously in 2004. In the period from May 2004 to March 2007, some 630,000 people from the eight accession states sought work in the UK.[2] This may seem a lot but, in proportion to the population, the figures for Ireland were even more impressive. Furthermore, the UK has for some time been a desired destination for foreign job seekers, and has traditionally been (at least in the cities) a multicultural society, so a couple of hundred thousand Eastern Europeans should not have represented a major challenge. (At least this is what most people thought before Brexit.) Other EU countries' job markets only followed after the so-called transition periods for the free movement of labour.

The Irish experience, however, has been quite different. Immigration there was a quite recent phenomenon and had come only a generation (or less) after Ireland began to recover from its own brain- and youth-drain. For centuries, Ireland used to be a country of emigration. 'Nobody ever wanted to come here', the Irish say. On the contrary, people just did not know how to get out quickly enough. The sight of so many now so eager to enter the country has been a source of both puzzlement and pride to the Irish – at least that was the case then. It was taking place in a society that was not really used to foreigners but also in one that – as I will try to show later on – shares some of the features with the societies of Eastern Europe.

It does not, therefore, come as a great surprise that Ireland (even before the 2008 recession hit the world) soon became perplexed about whether it was indeed a good idea to have workers from the new member states allowed in without work-permits. Initially, there was a general consensus that they had been a good thing for the Irish economy: they had mostly

---

2. Accession Monitoring Report, A8 Countries, May 2004 – March 2007, Home Office, May 2007.

taken jobs as construction workers, grocery shop assistants, or waiters and maids – jobs that are usually not particularly attractive to the 'natives'. But following some controversial cases, people began to wonder if workers from so-called Eastern Europe were indeed taking Irish jobs – despite the continued decline in unemployment.

It also soon became obvious that the lack of understanding of Eastern Europe and Eastern Europeans was becoming an issue. Even those – and they are the majority in Ireland – who do respect the dignity of immigrants have sometimes spoken about workers from Eastern Europe as if they were from an entirely different culture and required nothing less than an introduction to the ways of Europe. The rise of what today is seen as socially conservative policies and populism in Central and Eastern Europe has revived the need for such an introduction.

The issue of 'Eastern Europeans' in Ireland at the time had prompted me to start thinking about what it is that makes me feel European and why I – then a young diplomat in Ireland – am not comfortable with the label Eastern European, at least not when it is used, as it so often is, to imply a *Lesser* European. In fact, I had often felt like I woke up to a new world in 1990, when people in Western Europe started to call us by this uninspiring name – Eastern Europeans. As a famous Slovenian writer commented, Eastern Europe was created (again) with the European Enlargement Day of 2004. And the more we keep saying that this is not our name, the more it seems to be used.

Was I over-sensitive? A reviewer of the first edition of this book thought so and recommended that I should get over it, and accept the term Eastern Europe, then (as now) a common expression for the geopolitical region. Perhaps I should have done so, but questions over the character of the region and its roots remain.

Lack of knowledge of the Continent, and of Eastern Europe in particular, is not helpful when trying to understand Eastern Europeans on a temporary visit to Irish or English shores. Many of the older generation of Irish simply spoke of the whole of Eastern Europe as of 'Russia' – it was an alien, pagan and wrecked land. (On one occasion in 1958, when the Yugoslav regime put a Croatian Catholic bishop on trial, the bishop of Dublin warned the faithful against attending a scheduled football match against a team from Communist Yugoslavia – with little effect though.) The new generations do not always seem to have advanced in that respect all that much, since their ventures into the Continent are too often limited to sunny *playa* and cheap booze in one of the Eastern European capitals. The Irish, of course, are not alone in their attitudes. I have met many (too many) Italians who were not aware that their country has a common border with Slovenia, and low-cost airline stag-party trips of young Brits to Bratislava are not exactly signs of an enlightened search for the truth about Eastern Europe. Even closer to Eastern Europe, in Germany and Austria, the younger generation have lost all notion of the long-established links between the German-speaking world and the Slavs (an interaction to which I devote an entire chapter) that so much characterised the history of Europe. And in the Netherlands, another of my former postings, Eastern Europeans – including diplomats – continue to struggle hard to shake off all the negative stereotypes associated with the lands beyond the invisible *new* Berlin Wall. In the meantime, at least some Central European countries have, in the eyes of the Dutch, advanced to the category of *vakantieland*, an intriguing Dutch label hailing a country's touristic qualities. And I have not even touched upon the experience with Romanian workers in the Iberian Peninsula.

In 2004, the year of the accession of the eight new member states to the European Union, I was hoping in vain for a book to be written about Eastern Europe that would mark this truly remarkable event. At least in the English-speaking world, to my knowledge, no such book appeared on the history shelves of bookshops. Tourist guidebooks, seemingly unmoved and unimpressed by the big-bang enlargement, continued to feature Greece, which lies at the continent's south-easternmost edge, under the title of Western Europe and Slovenia, which lies west of Vienna, under the Eastern Europe section. So, I decided it was my turn to try to fill the gap.

Fast forward almost two decades, the ignorance has taken another, probably unexpected turn, and the gap between the two halves of Europe another character: that of perception of values. Or so it seems, calling for a fresh interpretation.

Indeed, the issue of the rule of law (to which I dedicate the final chapter), the attitudes to migration, views on the so-called 'sexual democracy' etc. have raised eyebrows in Brussels and in most of the Western capitals, especially with regards to Poland and Hungary. While some of these developments have more to do with an ordinary power-grab than ideology, it is essential to look at what is behind them – something that few if any analysts have dared to do. One of the key messages of this book is that these developments in the region have a lot to do with the political, social and cultural history of Central and Eastern Europe before World War II. This is, in short, what the first part of the book is about.

Part I: Setting the scene

St Ferghal and the Globalisation
of the Middle Ages

In 1994, in the small village of Vrhpolje in western Slovenia, only a dozen miles from the Italian border, there was a rather unusual public event, attended even by a high-ranking national politician. On a rock just outside the village, the villagers erected a monument, remembering a battle that took place exactly 1,600 years earlier between the Roman (Byzantine) Emperor Theodosius and the western usurper Eugenius. Although probably unknown to the reader, the battle was of considerable significance for European history, and the encounter is regarded as an important milestone in late Antiquity.[3]

The high profile of the celebration shows how even remote historical events are sometimes used by people in so-called Eastern Europe to claim the early participation of their lands (not even of their people in this case, as the Slavs would have not entered modern-day Slovenia until at least the sixth century!) in the development of the idea of Europe. One may

---

3. David Potter in *The Roman Empire at Bay* gives the battle at Frigidus, as it is usually referred to, a significance parallel to that of the battle at Adrianopolis. However, it seems symptomatic that Potter places the battle in northern Italy, whereas it actually took place in what is today Slovenia. Could it be that one has some difficulty in placing an important historical event in Eastern Europe? (Routledge, 2004, pp. 529–533).

find such attempts rather desperate, especially if they involve a 1,600-year-old battle. But something else is also striking: how is it possible that villagers living in a place less than two hours' drive away from Venice need so much to prove that they really belong to Europe? And what happened on the other side of the divide, in so-called Western Europe, to make territory only a few kilometres away seem so distant, so culturally different, that it deserves a special name – Eastern Europe?

Although the example of, say, the Czech Republic and Germany is very similar, the situation is particularly shocking when one looks at Slovenia and Italy. Except in the years immediately after World War II, there was never really an Iron Curtain between Italy and Slovenia. In 2004, on EU Enlargement Day, Western media, hungry for iconic images of the Iron Curtain, repeatedly used photo-shots of the rather unthreatening fence between Italian Gorizia/Gorica and Slovenian Nova Gorica, a kind of mini-Berlin Wall, but this was much to the amusement of the locals who were used to commuting daily through a nearby border post even in Communist times. (The purpose of that particular fence was more to mark the borderline than to prevent trespassing, and the most controversial event associated with it occurred in the 1950s, when a mob threw a high-ranking Slovenian clergyman over it into Italy, in an act masterminded by the Communist authorities.)

The truth was that, from the 1970s onwards, when Yugoslavia liberalised its border regime to allow for the development of its tourist industry and access to hard currency, Yugoslavs were free to travel anywhere they wished and as often as they wished. We were the privileged ones in the Communist world. Coming from a nearby town, I remember well how, in the years of my childhood, we used to go shopping in Italy almost every fortnight, bringing home items that were not available in Yugoslavia or were cheaper in Italy, like jeans, electronics, washing powder, fruits, coffee, etc.

I will return to the deeper significance of 'washing-powder tourism' later, but let me describe one more aspect of Cold War history at the border between Italy and Yugoslavia/Slovenia. Italians were also coming over to Slovenia in almost the same numbers to buy petrol and fresh meat or to indulge in Slovenian restaurants, casinos and good-value dental repairs. (In return, Yugoslav dinars, though not officially a convertible currency, were accepted in the shops of Trieste/Trst and Gorizia/Gorica.) However, those Italian shoppers, gamblers and patients seemed almost completely ignorant about the country (Slovenia) they were visiting. They seemed to know nothing of the centuries of shared history (except perhaps of *esuli,* the Italian refugees from Yugoslavia after World War II, and the *foibe* killing fields, to which I come later), as if Communist rule had simply erased them. In other words, during the Communist era it began to seem perfectly normal that Gorizia/Gorica or Trieste/Trst, with its Slovenian ethnic minority, should be labelled Western European, but that the immediate hinterland of Slovenia should be called an Eastern European land. And yet nobody was able to explain what exactly – other than Communism – made the Slovenian hinterland Eastern European and Trieste/Trst Western European.

In any account of European history, East and West first appear in connection with the Eastern and Western Roman Empire, i.e. the Byzantine Empire (called 'Roman' by Ottomans and Greeks and 'Greek' by the West) and the Latin Roman Empire (later referred to as the Frankish Empire). In 285 AD, the then Roman Emperor Diocletian moved the centre of the empire to the East and divided it in two, drawing the dividing line across the province of Illyricum (the name was later used also for Napoleon's occupied territories in the region) roughly where Bosnia and Herzegovina is today. This delimitation, with slight changes, continued to mark political divisions – albeit by new and different polities – right up until World War I. It also features prominently in Samuel Huntington's acclaimed work on the clash of civilisations.[4]

Diocletian's aim was certainly not to create Eastern Europe – he did not think of East and West in those terms, nor, of course, did he think of Europe. He decided to divide the great empire to improve its management and above all its protection against various barbarians, mostly Germanic tribes and peoples – in other words (ironically) future Europeans. Yet his choice of the division line was not purely arbitrary: he drew it where Latin influence faded and gave way to predominantly Greek influence. (The delimitation line was a couple of hundred miles east of *Castra ad Fluvium Frigidus*, the Roman outpost near modern Vrhpolje, the Slovenian village mentioned above.) The division only concerned Mediterranean Europe; the vast areas north of it, where today lie other regions that are part of Eastern Europe, were not included in this mapping, as they were out of Roman military control. As we shall see, the Greek half would later play a very important role in the formation of Eastern Europe.

In the times with which we are concerned at this point, Europe as a political entity did not yet exist but the Roman and Greek worlds – as the spiritual foundations of Europe – did. In fact, with the demise of the Western Roman Empire, it was the Byzantine Empire which took over the role of 'Europe'

---

4. Huntington, SP, *The Clash of Civilisations and the Remaking of the World Order,* The Free Press, 2002, pp. 157–161.

of the time. With Constantine, the capital of the Roman Empire was formally moved to the East. From then on, it was Byzantium, which regarded itself as the true Rome, as the 'world superpower', as 'Europe', and, as such, it continued to intervene militarily not only in the Apennine Peninsula (one of the most splendid achievements of Byzantine art can be found in Ravenna, an Italian city just south of Venice) and the Mediterranean, but also as far as the Iberian peninsula. And the power of Byzantium began to gain additional momentum once the pagan West had been subdued by barbarians. The city, known also as Constantinople, was at the heart of a Christian empire and it continued to flourish.

There have been ongoing attempts to define what made – or makes – Europe and its peoples European. The answer to this question proves not only to be far from obvious but also, and at the same time, highly divisive. In 2005, the draft European Constitution sparked some bitter exchanges on the issue of the role of Christianity in the formation of Europe. According to one of his close collaborators, Pope John Paul II wanted himself to intervene with the President of the Convention, Valéry Giscard d'Estaing, to have the Judaeo-Christian roots mentioned in the document too, but was discouraged from doing so.[5] In the end – and this appeared to be done under the strong influence of French views on the relationship between Church and State – only a vague reference to 'religious inheritance' remained in the preamble of a document that was later to be abandoned anyway. Indeed, it seemed that one of the biggest problems for those who framed the EU Constitution was to name the sources that inspired the listed European values (rights of

---

5. As quoted in Matzuzzi, M, *Il Santo Realismo: Il Vaticano come Potenza Politica Internazionale da Giovanni Paolo II a Francesco,* Luiss University Press 2021, p. 36.

the individual, freedom, democracy, equality and the rule of law, justice and solidarity, diversity, pride in national identity and history, etc). The preamble specifically mentioned only 'cultural, religious and humanist inheritance', but failed to say which religion(s) were referred to. It did, however, mention Humanism as a particular philosophical view. But, some asked, if Humanism is there, why not mention Christianity too? The usual explanation at the time was that mentioning one religion would discriminate against the others. The EU returned to this debate with the Lisbon Treaty, but Christianity fared no better and animosity to, or at least unease about its Christian roots, as we shall see later, has continued to haunt Europe to the present day. Worse, doubts began to emerge about Europe's Humanistic roots too.

Some Eastern Europeans, notably the Poles, were particularly unhappy about this disregard for Christianity. The truth is that Humanism, which *was* mentioned, could only have taken root in an originally Christian environment. Moreover, it was mostly a Western and Central European phenomenon. In 'Eastern Europe proper' (i.e. Orthodox Eastern Europe), Humanism only made an appearance from the late eighteenth century, and was even then seen as a Western importation. For an important part of Eastern Europe then, it was Christianity (or Christendom) which provided the basic link with the rest of the Continent.[6] At risk of some over-simplification, here too

---

6. 'In the prevailing narrative of European identity, "Europe" as an idea took shape only in the Middle Ages, when it succeeded the concept of Christendom. Both are Western: indeed, Christendom is often qualified as "Western Christendom". In this narrative of Europe, Byzantium is conspicuously absent. In historiography about the expanding (Western) Europe in the centuries after 1000, with its eastward adventures, Byzantium has usually featured as an ambivalence, less an ally than a duplicitous threat.' Quoted from Averil Cameron, *The Byzantines,* Blackwell, p. 165.

lies a good part of the underlying causes of the spat between Brussels on one hand, and Poland and Hungary on the other, as I shall elaborate in more detail in the second part of this book

Christianisation (or the creation of Christendom) was a cultural, political and also 'technological' and military process, a sort of globalisation of the early Middle Ages. The Western Roman Empire did not really care about it and disappeared; the Eastern Empire embraced it and survived much longer. The Roman (Western) legacy was taken over by the Franks, who did recognise the political value of Christianity, while the Eastern Empire took over some of the legacy of the ancient Greeks. Thus, in the early Middle Ages, the Frankish Empire and the Byzantine Empire each stood at its own end of the European continent, fighting to subdue – in a political and religious sense – the peoples in-between, above all the Slavs, who entered Europe about that time and who were to become central to what would be known as Eastern Europe.

What was at stake for these early 'Eastern Europeans' in this process? Of major political importance in the region at that time were two peoples: the Bulgars, i.e. the early Bulgarians (actually of non-Slav origin) and the Moravians (that is to say, the ancestors of the Czechs and the Slovaks), and both sought to manoeuvre between the two superpowers of the day, the Byzantine Empire and the Franks. Contrary to what geographical position might suggest, the Bulgars first sought Christian missionaries from the Franks, and the Moravians from Byzantium. The Bulgars' approach to the Franks was not well received by the Byzantines and Constantinople reacted militarily. The final solution to what was, at first examination, a religious issue was reached at the ecumenical council in Constantinople where a majority of Eastern bishops decided that Bulgarians should fall under the religious rule of Constantinople rather than Rome. This left a profound mark on Bulgaria for the rest of its history: it acquired the Greek-influenced Cyrillic script and it remained in the realm of what later came to be known as Orthodox Christianity. The move also facilitated the Christianisation of Russians – the so-called Kiev Russians, i.e. the early ancestors of modern Russians and Ukrainians, who accepted Christianity in 987 AD. This lies at the roots of the preposterous Russian claims over Ukraine, which try to justify the recent aggression. In the now already infamous essay by Putin, *On the Historical Unity of Russians and Ukrainians* in July of 2021, seven months before the invasion, Putin claimed that Russians, Ukrainians and Belarus were one single people and that 'true sovereignty of Ukraine is possible only in partnership with Russia'.[7]

In Moravia, the arrival of two Greek preachers, Cyril (also known as Constantine) and Methodius, challenged the plans of Frankish missionaries and politicians. Under some pressure, the disciples of these two brothers were expelled and Moravia, together with Carantania to the south (a principality of early Slovenians that covered roughly the same territory as the Austrian province of Carinthia today), came under Bavarian political influence. The Bavarians themselves had already been subdued by the Franks, converted about the same time as Slovenians. Christianisation was interrupted for a while by the arrival of the Avars (one of the ancestors of the Magyars) but Frankish help to the Slavs as they defended themselves against the new arrivals tightened the Bavarian/Frankish grip. After a brief but very important Irish mission (St Ferghal was bishop of Salzburg and

---

7. https://en.wikisource.org/wiki/On_the_Historical_Unity_of_Russians_and_Ukrainians

he is still regarded as the Apostle of the Carantanians, i.e. the early Slovenians), Carantanians as well as other Slavs in Central Europe came under Germanic ecclesiastical control.

Further to the north, the early Bohemian rulers were looking westward too. Magdeburg became the centre for the Christianisation of western Slavs. In 964, Poles acquired Christianity from Bohemians through royal marriage. Later on, Poles and Czechs would be among the few Slavic nations able to establish their own church provinces directly reporting to Rome, which would enable them to maintain, at least for some time, a fair degree of political independence.

The Hungarians, one of the non-Slavic nations of Eastern Europe, initially came under Greek influence but German clergy prevailed after AD 980. Christianity was thus firmly established in the whole of Eastern Europe by the early years of the eleventh century. The exception was Lithuania, which only ceased to be formally pagan in 1385 when, again through marriage, its rulers accepted the Roman Catholic faith from Poles.

Without going into too much detail and for the purpose of our further discussion, it is important to note that Europe, in these early centuries in the form of the Christendom of Charlemagne, already included a great part of what today is popularly called Eastern Europe. By the fourteenth century, when 'Europe' got an even better defined shape and the Holy Roman Empire of the German Nation (a union of small principalities that were mostly but not exclusively German-speaking and that much later gave birth to what is today known as Germany) was firmly established, the political inclusion of the vast majority of modern Eastern Europe was even more evident.

Of course, there was no Western or Eastern Europe in the time of Charlemagne. To the Franks, the Slavs and Magyars were simply those (usually violent) invaders that needed to be dealt with in some way. Christianisation – even though in part carried out at sword-point – was a surprisingly civilised method of containing the Slavic (and later Magyar) menace, at least by the standards of the early Middle Ages. In some way, it was akin to the enlargement process of the European Union. To Christianise Slavs also meant turning them into allies, and allies – at least Christian allies – do not fight against each other. This stopped the advance of the Slav hordes but also made violence against them, now they were Christian, less acceptable morally. The new alliances also implied that, sooner or later, since they were at a lower level of political organisation, Slavs would be subdued by those who had already achieved a higher version of statehood, as the Franks had. It would, of course, be very premature to see in this any form of nationalism: the world of Charlemagne was not a world of ethnicities and even less so one of nations. It was a simple fact that, at a point when Christianity was gaining popularity, the Franks (as proto-Germans or proto-French or proto-Europeans) were at a stage of political organisation which allowed the use (and misuse) of Christian religion for political purposes. For the Slavs to opt for Christianity may have meant an uncertain political future (although would there be any more certainty in confronting the Franks militarily?) but it also meant becoming a part of 'Europe'; a part of the globalisation of the Middle Ages.

One can only speculate about how much this globalisation was controversial at the time. How far the decision to accept Christianity was a conscious one is difficult to say, even for the Slavic rulers.[8] On the other hand, some historians believe

---

8. Averil Cameron in *The Byzantines* writes that the Russian Vladimir's choice of Christianity was only made after '...research about the merits of Islam, Roman Catholicism and the Orthodoxy represented by Byzantium'. Ibid., p. 173.

that it was not all about worldly interests, and that leaders such as Charlemagne were guided by genuine religious zeal.[9]

The fact is that, culturally speaking, Christianisation gave the Slavs the first written texts in their own languages, facilitated access to the 'science' and arts of the day (at least to those very few at the time who could read and write) and generally brought them into the family of Christian nations, a sort of EU of the day. To expand the Kingdom of God in a faster and easier way, the missionaries made use of teaching and preaching in the vernacular, which also meant that these languages were given more defined written forms and were, ultimately, able to survive into the present day. The Freising Manuscripts, from the tenth and eleventh centuries, for example, which were written in early Slovenian, became the oldest written texts in any Slavic language in the Latin alphabet.

Twentieth-century historiography, as revised by the Communist authorities after World War II, tried to portray Christianisation primarily as the political subjugation of Slavs by Germans. But while it is true that Slavs – with the possible exceptions of the Poles and the Czechs – lagged behind Western Europe in terms of political organisation and were politically subdued by the Germans, they did manage to survive as distinct ethnic groups until the present day. The fact that they were included in the family of Christian nations (with all the political consequences that followed this) certainly did help to prevent them being wiped out as pagans, which was the fate of some peoples of early medieval Europe who persisted in their pagan beliefs and practices.

---

9. Derek Wilson, *Charlemagne, The Great Adventure* (Hutchinson, London 2005).

By around the thirteenth century therefore, what today we call Eastern Europe was almost fully included in Christendom – the 'Europe' of the day. But there was one important distinction within the region: the peoples or ethnic groups of Eastern Europe, who received Christianity from Constantinople, adopted the Greek version of it, together with the Greek script (later developed into Cyrillic) and they accepted cultural and political influence from Byzantium. By contrast, Slovenians, Croats, Slovaks, Hungarians, Czechs and Poles received Christianity largely from the German church (and also, to a much lesser extent, from the Latin lands of modern northern Italy) and, consequently, they have adopted Latin script, Western thought and Western political organisation.

Eastern Europe proper was thus born out of the schism in the Church, the split that also occurred because of the political rivalry between the Byzantines and the Franks over the bodies and souls of the Slavs. However, this was not the same Eastern Europe that we know today; it was certainly not called 'Eastern Europe' then. At the head of medieval 'Eastern Europe' was Greece which was surrounded by nations that had adopted the rites of Greek Christianity like the Serbs, the Bulgarians and the early Russians. Further west and north, however, there was another 'Eastern' Europe which used Western Christian rites. From this time to the present day, these two divisions of Eastern Europe have followed quite distinct paths. No wonder that, in the Middle Ages, no one thought of the Czechs or Slovenians as Eastern Europeans.

If any evaluation of this kind is possible, one could say that the nations in the Middle Ages which chose the Eastern rite and Byzantine influence did not, in any way, make a bad decision.[10] Quite the contrary: first, the choice was not a voluntary one but was a result of geographical proximity and/or *realpolitik*. Second, and more importantly, until about the eleventh century, Byzantium surpassed the Western European kingdoms and empires in almost every respect: culturally, economically and militarily. In fact, one of the reasons why Diocletian moved the centre of gravity of the empire to the East was that this part was much more civilised and prosperous.[11] People of Byzantium looked down on the then recently converted barbarians in the west. For political leaders of 'Eastern Europe' in the Middle Ages, attachment to Byzantium rather than the West might well have looked more attractive for some very good reasons.

It is also interesting to note another factor: while the countries of today's Eastern Europe were certainly not at the core of Europe in the Middle Ages, they were by no means far from it. Economically speaking, historians talk about the axis of medieval Europe, drawn roughly from Antwerp (or later London) to Florence. For a very long time, this was the area of the most intense economic activity, enabled by fertile valleys, navigable rivers, access to the sea, dense population, and large cities. Looking at the map, one can see that the Czech lands, Slovenia, Slovakia, Hungary and Poland did not really lie far from these centres of medieval Europe and were certainly not further from it than Spain, Portugal or Ireland. In fact, until

10. It was much later that the term Byzantine was (wrongly) assigned a negative meaning. Averil Cameron in *The Byzantines* notes that the *Oxford English Reference Dictionary* explains the term with 'extremely complicated, inflexible or carried on by underhand means'. ibid., p. 3. The same author also draws attention to the fact that even Byzantine studies, as an academic discipline, continue to be discriminated against. (see p. 5).
11. For more details on the supremacy of Byzantium see Warren Treadgold, *A Concise History of Byzantium,* Palgrave, 2001.

about AD 1000, economic activity was pretty basic all over Europe. Distinguished British economist Angus Maddison, known for his calculations of historic economic performance, has estimated the GDP of Europe in those days as 400 dollars per capita,[12] both in the East and the West. The European economy only really took off after the year 1000 and it is about that time that Western and Eastern Europe slowly began to diverge economically. For the year 1500, the same author has made the following estimates for GDP per capita (expressed in the same 1990 international dollars and for the territories of present-day countries): Austria 707, Finland 453, France 727, Germany 688, Italy 1,100, the Netherlands 761, Norway 640, Sweden 695, Switzerland 632, the UK 714, Ireland 526, Greece 433, Portugal 606 and Spain 661. Unfortunately, the author presented only one, uniform figure for the entire Eastern Europe – 496 dollars. Although we can probably assume that, in the year 1500, the GDP of Central European countries was higher than in the Ottoman-occupied areas or in the sparsely populated areas of Eastern Europe 'proper', the gap between the East and West was beginning to show. On the other hand, we can also see that the economy was poor in other fringe lands as well, such as modern-day Ireland, Finland and Greece.

The Czechs, the Hungarians and the Poles (less so the 'unhistorical' nations such as the Slovenes) developed impressive enough political structures in the Middle Ages, comparable with what existed in the west. For example, the medieval Bohemian (Czech) kings were among the key political players in Europe of the time. (Think of the magnificent

---

12. Angus Maddison, *The World Economy: Historical Statistics* (OECD, 2003). The GDP per capita is estimated taking the 1990 world economy as the measuring stick. Consequently, the calculated 'currency' is called '1990 international Geary-Khamis dollars'.

Karlštejn castle of Emperor Charles IV.) Later the reformation movement of the Czech Jan Hus preceded that of Luther, and the Czechs were at the centre of the all-European political and religious dispute that caused the so-called Thirty Years' War, after which they were finally subdued by the Habsburgs. All in all, although political, social and economic development in parts of Eastern Europe in the Middle Ages began lagging behind that of mainstream Western Europe after the year 1000, there was little then to suggest a general backwardness of the region – and nothing that suggested a distinct name was required for this part of Europe.

The Slavs and the Rest
of the Eastern Europeans

On our short journey through the history of Eastern Europe we now move from late antiquity to early middle ages. Things turned sour for Europe in the sixth century with the arrival of the Slavs, feared by both Germanic people and by the Byzantines. We do not know for sure whether violence against the old settlers (Germanic peoples, Greeks, Romans and other Romanised native peoples) was the dominant pattern when the Slavs moved in. There are also suggestions that, at least in some instances, they integrated into existing societies culturally, even when they prevailed ethnically. In any event they drew another wedge between the Franks and the Byzantines, obstructing the lines of communication between the two civilisations and the two superpowers of the day.[13]

With their arrival, Slavs became the dominant element in Eastern Europe and they have been so ever since, despite the fact that there are a number of non-Slav peoples in Eastern Europe: none of the peoples of the Baltic nations is Slav, nor are the Hungarians, the Romanians or the Albanians. The Greeks – the ultimate Eastern Europeans – are not Slavs.

---

13. For more details on the nature of the Slav (and others) migration see Peter Heather, *Empires and Barbarians,* Macmillan, 2009, pp. 386–451.

Nor can the (mostly Slavic) world east of the former Iron Curtain be simply reduced to a Russian influence zone, despite Russia's crucial (and sometimes brutal) role in the region in modern history. In fact, Russia only significantly entered the general history of Eastern Europe at quite a late date, not much before the reign of Peter the Great in the last decades of the seventeenth century. (Although Lithuanians and Poles, who had established a commonwealth which was a key player in the region stretching from the Baltic to the Black Sea in the Middle Ages, were at loggerheads with their Eastern neighbours centuries earlier.) Peter the Great started building cultural ties with Western Europe at much the same time as he also began his territorial expansion to the West, with the Poles, the Baltic nations and the Finns being its first victims. From then on, Russia would continue to be seen as a threat to them.

After Christianisation, Poles and Czechs continued to enjoy relative political autonomy. This was not the case for Slovenians, who were soon submerged into Charlemagne's empire, or for Slovaks who came under Magyar rule. Further south-east, Serbs and Bulgarians too had their medieval states. For the south-eastern Slavs, the Greeks and some other nations in this part of Europe, however, the end of political autonomy came with the beginning of the Ottoman conquest of European territory in the fourteenth century. This also shook the Hungarian kingdom and the lands of the Moldavians and the Wallachians, the ancestors of Romanians. The period of Ottoman rule and its key significance for this part of Eastern Europe will be looked at closely in a separate chapter. For now, it is important to realise that the centuries of Ottoman rule (which, despite occasional uprisings, were largely peaceful times) somehow froze the history of south-eastern Europe until the nineteenth century when the Ottoman Empire began to collapse and Russia also started to exercise a stronger influence in the region.

The crumbling Ottoman Empire made possible the Russian advance towards the Black Sea and the Mediterranean. This went hand-in-hand with the rise of several, mostly (but not solely) Slavic and Orthodox Christian nations in parts of the falling Ottoman Empire. Thus the new Eastern question – who was to get the spoils from the final wars against the dying Ottoman Empire? – enabled Russia to gain a stronger influence in Eastern Europe. This was made easier by the common Slavic and religious (Orthodox Christian) roots of the Russians and of some of the liberated Slavs. Shared Slavic origins continued to appeal even to the Catholic Slavs of the West, like the Czechs and the Slovenians, who, at least at certain points in their history, saw in Russia a beacon of Slavic power and might, and an inspiration against the rising German nationalism of the late nineteenth century, even when there was no physical contact with the Russians. The so-called Pan-Slavic campaign, a nineteenth-century patriotic movement emphasising the unity of all Slavs, drew on the even older sources of the two preachers, the brothers Constantine and Methodius. Although the two were Greeks and not Slavs, they continued to be known as the Apostles of the Slavs even in Catholic countries. Their feast according to the Catholic calendar is still a public holiday in the Czech Republic, which is otherwise rather reserved on the topic of shared Slavic roots and, in any event, one of the most secularised societies in Europe.

The Pan-Slavic movement remained more or less on the level of an idea, with little practical consequences, but, even in the twentieth century, various Slovenian religious and patriotic societies bore the name of the two Greek brothers and today they are still associated with the Christian ecumenical movement.

Not all of the Slavic countries embraced the Pan-Slavic idea with the same enthusiasm, which reflects not only the sometimes controversial nature of such associations within the Slavic world, but also the variety of historical experiences that individual Eastern European countries (and Slavic countries among them) have had with Russia. Slovenia, on the other hand, is less troubled by such anxieties because there has never been a Russian military presence on Slovenian soil. (The only two exceptions are Russian prisoners of war held there during World War I and World War II, and the brief presence of the Red Army in the north-eastern corner of Slovenia, formerly occupied by Hungary, immediately after World War II.) Nurturing this, at surface, wholly non-controversial relationship was thus something that Slovenian politicians thought could only complement the country's main orientation towards the EU and NATO. Russians thought differently. A wooden World War I Orthodox chapel, built by Russian (and other) prisoners of war under Mt. Vršič, was relatively uncontroversial but the issue of World War II military presence has been less straightforward. Throughout the 2010s, the Russian government was zealously pursuing a campaign of erecting memorials to the Red Army soldiers at every possible location, amounting to what some saw as part of the imposition of a geopolitical narrative by President Putin – politically marking the territory. In any even scarce historical links with Russia were thus suddenly disproportionally represented in Slovenia. Other Eastern European countries, whose relationships with Russia have been, at best, ambivalent both in the past and the present, were particularly wary of such advances of Russian public diplomacy – they rather saw it as a part of hybrid warfare. During my years in Prague, the city borough of Prague 6 was engulfed in a conflict with the Russian embassy over the memorial to the Soviet Marshal Konev who led the army of the Soviet liberators of Prague in 1945. Konev infamously returned to Prague in 1968, on a much less noble mission. He had also been involved in the suppression of the Budapest uprising in 1956. It was this post-World War II engagement of his that eventually led the local authority to remove his statue in 2020, despite the protests of the Russian embassy and the local communist party. Similarly, at the height of Russian aggression in Ukraine in the summer of 2022, Estonia decided to remove Soviet-era monuments, arguing that this is the way to prevent 'tearing open old wounds'. Keeping Russian memorials in public spaces became an issue of internal security, especially in Russian-populated areas of the country.[14]

One could speculate that, had it not been for the imposed Soviet domination of Central and Eastern Europe after World War II, the Russian language would spontaneously have become the *lingua franca* of the region. Indeed, I always feel strange resorting to English in order to speak to my Czech, Slovak or Polish friends. Speaking Russian, one of the great Slavic languages, would somehow be more natural. Some of the Czechs, Slovaks and Poles (at least those that went to school before 1990) may still be able to communicate in Russian but would usually refuse to do so because they regard it as the language of the former 'oppressor' – a sad fate for the native language of such great European spirits as Tolstoy, Dostoevsky, Solzhenitsyn and many others.

---

14. Estonia removes Soviet-era tank memorial over Russian tensions, *Financial Times*, 16 August 2022.

Thus more than 30 years after the fall of the Berlin Wall, Russian feels rather unusable – except with the Russian population in the Baltics. As a result, most Eastern Europeans today prefer to use English. Similarities between Slavic languages naturally continue to exist, though they do not offer the same kind of closeness as Swedish, Norwegian and Danish. Language-wise too, Eastern Europe is as diverse as its Western counterpart.

But contrary to the positive stereotypes of Romanic nations (Spaniards, French, Italian, Portuguese) who are associated with good food, easy living, sensuality and style and Germanic nations, linked with technical superiority and enterprise, Slavic nations are, at best, associated with folklore and, at worst, with shabbiness and misery. Prized movies from Slavic Eastern Europe usually deal with issues like discrimination against the Roma community, ethnic conflicts, the trafficking of people and so on – undoubtedly valid and relevant themes but not an exact reflection of ordinary, everyday life in this part of Europe. It seems that the juries at international film festivals show less interest in general, human themes or even in the issues of social change that transition has brought to Eastern Europe, resulting in a self-censorship effect on Eastern European scriptwriters and directors who seem to have discovered that stereotypes are easier to sell.

It is probably for similar reasons that people seem to find the politics of Eastern Europe just too difficult to comprehend. Again and again I read about the long history of violent conflicts in Eastern Europe, about a 'troubled' region, but I find it hard to think of any truly major conflict, before the wars in the former Yugoslavia or the Russian aggression against Ukraine. The history of this part of Europe offers nothing on the scale of the conflicts between the French and the Germans, or the British and the French or the various civil wars which have plagued Western Europe. There were no Napoleons in Eastern Europe before Stalin (except Napoleon himself for a brief period of time), and the nations of Eastern Europe have lived in relative harmony with one another over the centuries.

Before the twentieth century, wars in Eastern Europe were mostly fought with Russians, Ottomans and the ancestors of modern Hungarians; the latter came into the region after the Slavs and were soon seen as fearsome warriors. They populated a vast area, previously occupied by the Slavs, and were only finally halted by joint Slav and Frankish forces. If it had not been for the Hungarians, who ended up living between the lands of the Slovenians and the Slovaks, people in Western Europe today would probably be less likely to mix up the two nations. According to linguists, there are very important similarities between the Slovenian and the Slovak languages (although these similarities are not so strong that I don't have to resort to English when I speak to my Slovakian friends!). Looking on the map, one can see only a relatively short stretch of Austria (part of the country which contains a Croatian-speaking minority) lying between the extreme north-eastern corner of Slovenia and the extreme south-west of Slovakia, confirming the ancient connection. (In fact, after World War I, the peace conference in Paris briefly contemplated the idea of using this stretch of land as a corridor, politically linking what were then Czechoslovakia and Yugoslavia.[15])

Slav suspicions of Hungarians were reciprocated by the Hungarians. With Finns and Estonians as their closest and nearest ethnic relatives, Hungarians always felt like an isolated island in a Slavic sea, and they also felt threatened by

---

15. MacMillan, p. 246

Romanians and Austrians. Anxious to reach out from their isolation, they looked to the south, for access to the Adriatic Sea, and Croatia was indeed once included in their Kingdom. When Bosnia was annexed by Austria-Hungary in 1908, they tried in vain to have it for themselves. And it was Hungary which, more than German-speaking Austria, most fiercely opposed the creation of a third, Slavic unit (in addition to the Austrian and Hungarian ones) in the Austro-Hungarian Empire, fearful of reducing their bargaining power versus the Austrians. Finally, the end of World War I saw Hungarian territory, in accordance with the Treaty of Trianon, reduced to a third of its pre-war size, including sizable portions of its ethnic Hungarian areas. Such was the scale of this loss, that it continues to be the cause of national mourning 100 years later – and at the same time something that Mr Orbán can still use to rally support. I shall return to this topic later.

With such an eloquent history, Hungary stands out among the nations of Eastern Europe as probably the one that has had its own sovereign state for the longest time. Of course, this state took different forms and shapes over the centuries, and periods of sovereign rule were interrupted by shorter or longer periods of foreign domination, but overall Hungarians have the strongest tradition of statehood in the region. They are followed closely by the Poles. Croats and Serbs had powerful early medieval kingdoms which later disappeared. Serbs and Bulgarians only regained independence in the nineteenth century, as did the Greeks. Czechs finally lost their independence to Habsburgs in the seventeenth century. Most of Eastern Europe, as we shall see later, only fully regained its independence in the early twentieth century, as a result of the break-up of either the Ottoman Empire or Austria-Hungary. Indeed, for Central Europe, the experience of the

Austro-Hungarian Empire, lasting 500 years, was central and has decisively shaped the region's political, social and cultural history. Its long endurance was another reason for the absence of any major conflict among the peoples of Eastern Europe.

But there *was* a major conflict involving the nations of Eastern Europe – the one with the Ottoman Empire. The arrival of Ottomans and their long-lasting rule in South-Eastern Europe was actually the second event after the Christian schism between the Orthodox and Catholic Church to alter the shape of Eastern Europe, creating another, third tier in the region – the Balkans. Central Europe was affected too: while busy fending off the occasional Ottoman inroads, it was unable to make a fuller grasp of the Renaissance. The Byzantine Empire, the Orthodox part of Eastern Europe, played the key role in this conflict; it also created a special bond with Slavic peoples, and this is why I turn to it next.

The Byzantine Empire and Orthodox Eastern Europe 'Proper'

In the Catholic Church the last couple of decades have seen increased efforts to reach out to the Orthodox world. This interest in things Orthodox intensified with the late Pope John Paul II, who was very impressed by the spirituality of the Eastern Churches and, in particular, by the veneration of Mary in the Orthodox tradition.

This seems to be somehow at odds with the baroque features of Central Europe. In fact, John Paul II's interest in things Orthodox may be equally confusing for those trying to understand Eastern Europe. His homeland Poland, like the rest of Central Europe, is traditionally Catholic, not Orthodox. His own comments from the balcony of St Peter's on the very day of his election that he had come from 'a far land' did not help either. (His native city of Krakow is actually closer to Rome than Berlin, but at the time of his election in 1978 it definitely felt distant in space and time.) His interest in Eastern spirituality was, above all, religious, though some think that he was also concerned about mending the uneasy relationship that has existed between Russians and Poles through the centuries and, of course, between the Orthodox and the Catholic Church – something that is dear to Pope Francis too. Deep down, the interest of the late Slav pope in things Orthodox was also a result of the fact that he was a

Slav himself and that an important part of the Slav world is Orthodox.

In striving to be everything to everyone, Western Christianity (above all the Protestant churches, but also the Catholic Church) has gone to great lengths to strip itself of those elements that are conditioned by national cultures and old traditions, and which are not strictly related to religion as such. Churches started to use not only the vernacular but also plain everyday language. They absolved believers of the need for undue ceremonials, excessive piety and unnecessary regulations. Much, though not all, of the Church's 'red tape' has gone. Religion and its liturgies lie barer than ever before. This is certainly the case in the Catholic Church in English-speaking countries where the influence of the Anglican Church and the long disenfranchisement of the Catholic Church have made the interiors of the churches and the liturgy much simpler than they are in Central Europe where the appeal of the baroque is still strong.[16] Similar trends can be seen in Germany and the Netherlands.

But as a result of this 'depletion', some in the Catholic Church have begun to show greater interest in Orthodox Christianity and its spirituality, rich in ritual, lengthy ceremonies, incomprehensible ancient texts and holy pictures.

Others – out of similar motives – have opted for a revived interest in the Latin mass.[17] And not only that: across Europe

16. An excellent account of this transformation of the Catholic Church in an English setting is contained in the hilarious *How Far Can You Go?* by David Lodge, Penguin Books 1981.

17. Paradoxically, Pope Benedict XVI who had some sympathy for this Latin mass revival at the same time very much emphasised rationality in the Catholic faith, as expressed in his address at Regensburg in September 2006, which sparked so much indignation amongst Muslims. On the other side, Pope Francis issued instructions that severely limit the possibilities

and the US, some Catholics, clergy and laity alike, are turning away from what they see as a liberal relativism seeping into the Church. In their eyes, the conclusion of the Second Vatican Council provided a Catholic equivalent for such doctrinal backsliding. Thus conservatism is on the rise in many quarters within the Catholic Church all over the world, though in many places facing opposition by moderate and liberal Catholics. In Poland, a conservative position, fuelled by strong Catholic tradition, an urban-rural divide and conspiracy theories helped replace the political liberal elite and sustains on the surface the Law and Justice Party of Mr Kaczyński. This put Poland on a path that within a decade led to a collision with the European liberal mainstream. I shall elaborate this in more detail in the final chapter, but at this stage it is important to understand the religious factors behind these political developments.

What later become the Orthodox Church approached the Slavs with a tailor-made scripture based on the Greek alphabet – Glagolitic, and then with the Cyrillic script, which both have special characters for some of the sounds found in the early Slavic languages. These scripts seemed better suited for writing down the Slavic languages. Indeed, in some ways, it could be said that Orthodox Christianity in general seems 'more Slavic', as it holds memories of the primordial unity of Slavs in the times of Constantine and Methodius. By the same token, the Slavs of Central Europe (Slovenians, Croats, Slovaks, Czechs, Poles) are somehow 'less Slav' than those further east, as their identity has also a strong imprint of the Germanic (and Latin) world – a subject I will deal with in the following chapter.

---

for celebrating the Latin mass, which he saw as an outer manifestation of the conservative strand in the Catholic Church, opposing the reforms of the Second Vatican Council.

As we can see, Eastern Europe too is religiously and culturally divided between its own East and West, though there are still visible traces of the bond that once linked the two in a single Slavic entity. While the majority of Orthodox peoples are Slav, there are exceptions. The Romanians and the Greeks are two Orthodox nations that are not Slavic, and the Romanians have a further distinction – not only do they write in a Latin script, they also speak a Latin language, the closest you can get to Italian anywhere in the world. There is more than religion and script when it comes to things Orthodox!

After the fall of the Western Roman Empire, the Eastern Empire used to be referred to simply as the Roman Empire, which reflected the fact that it regarded itself (rightfully so, as we saw in the first chapter) as the real heir to Rome and as the (only) true defender of the Christian faith. It only began to be called 'Byzantium' after its fall in 1453; it got the name from a small town near Constantinople/Istanbul. (Interestingly, in some Slavic languages such as Slovenian, it is still called 'Carigrad', that is, the city of the Tsar or Emperor.)

While over the centuries Byzantium was more or less able to subdue or contain the military threat of the Bulgarians and the Slavs, their Muslim adversaries had gradually emerged as their most dangerous enemies. In addition, Byzantium was a theocratic state, its leaders taking theological issues very seriously – as seriously as perhaps only Charlemagne did in the West. Gradually this became a political problem in its relations with the West, where the papacy grew more and more distant from Constantinople – and vice versa. Increasingly, the Holy Roman Empire on one hand and the Roman Empire of Constantinople on the other became irrelevant to each other in both a political and a religious sense. The preoccupation of Byzantium with the Slavs and later with the Arabs and the Ottomans, as well as the physical barriers (the wedge of Slavs between the two empires) exacerbated the problem. The theological differences were further complicated by disagreement over the Crusades. Ultimately, Byzantium was sacked by the Crusaders in 1204, which is still an issue for the Orthodox Church even today. There were attempts to restore the empire and the union of the Church but, with only reluctant help offered by the West against the Ottomans, often conditional on doctrinal alignment, Byzantium never really recovered. It was finally defeated by the Ottomans in 1453 and became Istanbul.

The later developments are the subject of the next chapter, which will show that it was during the Ottoman era that the term 'Eastern' finally began to take root, although in a rather different sense than the modern use of it would imply. It is important to understand that, in the early Middle Ages up until the twelfth or even the thirteenth century, there was nothing 'Eastern' (meaning 'lesser') about the Byzantine Empire. Quite the contrary: the world then was Byzantium-centric. Europe's periphery was defined in relation to the Byzantine Empire, and it was Charlemagne and the popes who were trying hard to change this, first by the use of titles and language and then by *realpolitik*. It was only after about 1000 AD that Byzantium began slowly to decline, mainly because of its problems with the Arabs and later with the Ottomans. However, the association of Byzantium with bad government is mostly an invention. There is nothing in its history to suggest that 'standards in public office' in Byzantium were any lower than those in contemporary Western Europe. It is, therefore, erroneous to cite the Byzantine origins of Eastern Europe as a contributing factor to the relative backwardness of Eastern Europe in later centuries.

What was different – as already suggested – was the relationship between the Church and the State. In the West, worldly rulers were busy thinking about how they could use the Church for their own political purposes. On the other hand, the Church, although it was eager to influence politics and even ran its own state, was busy fighting for its own independence, in particular in ecclesiastical nominations and on property. From today's perspective, it may seem that in the past the Church ruled the West, hand-in-hand with the secular powers. But this was only really true where and when it suited the latter and, despite many exceptions to the rule, the ideal of the separation of the clerical and the secular spheres of activity is intrinsic to Western Christianity. When the Church in the West interfered with politics, it tried to do so on its own terms. It did not allow secular rulers to deal with theological issues. This was not the same in the Orthodox world where there was no attempt to conceal the unity of the two powers, sacred and secular. In fact, this unity was promoted and seen as a virtue, not primarily as an opportunity for political manipulation. Many rulers were genuinely concerned about theological issues and regarded themselves in the first instance as defenders of the faith. They also sincerely believed that the Christian God would punish them and destroy their earthly power if they did not uphold the true (Orthodox) Christian faith and lead their subjects to Him. Christianity was more important than the State. Of course, this is a generalisation and not all the Byzantine rulers were as devoted. But, in the West, the Church, with its own State and an effective religious infrastructure, was, from early in its history, a power in its own right and it was secular rulers who needed the Church to provide validation of their rule. In other words, in the West, the Church was independent of the State, although the reverse was not necessarily the case. In the Byzantine world, it was not: the Church and the State were more or less the same and this was seen as a strength and a virtue.[18]

This relationship between politics and religion in the Orthodox world led to the creation of national Churches and also to a degree of isolation from the rest of the world. It also enabled Orthodox nations to survive Ottoman rule by means of semi-autonomous structures within the Ottoman state when Byzantium (and other lands in the Balkans) was conquered by the Ottomans. But Ottoman rule also meant that these Orthodox Churches and their respective societies were 'protected' from (or deprived of) the influence of Reformation and the Enlightenment, which together with Christianity were of central importance for the formation of Western civilisation.[19] Even today, this ethnocentrism (or nationalism) of Orthodox Churches remains one of its key problems, echoing in politics in Montenegro, North Macedonia and Ukraine. In all these cases, newly independent nations had to invest a lot

---

18. See for example Bertrand Russell: 'In the Eastern Church, the patriarch of Constantinople never acquired either that independence of secular authority or that superiority to other ecclesiastics that was achieved by the pope.' (*The History of Western Philosophy*, Simon & Schuster, p. 390).

19. Averil Cameron writes that it was with the Ottoman conquest of south-eastern Europe that the region was closed off from the intellectual developments that had existed within Byzantine society and led to the 'permanent identification of Byzantium with absolutism on the one hand and Orthodox spirituality on the other. The negativity that surrounds the idea of Byzantium is especially evident in the modern discourse of "balkanism", and the idea of "byzantinism", or "byzantinismus" plays an important part among the negative characteristics that mark out the Balkans from "Europe" and "the West".' See Cameron, pp.175–76. For more on the image of the Balkans see Maria Todorova's seminal work, *Imagining the Balkans*.

of energy to get an ecclesiastical acknowledgement of their independence, contested by other Orthodox nations with their own national Orthodox churches.

What about the relationship of Byzantium with the rest of Eastern Europe? Byzantine influence was limited to the south-east and the far east of Europe – it never managed to establish itself in the areas of modern Hungary, Poland or the Czech Republic, i.e. Central Europe. The centre of the Byzantine world was originally, of course, Greece, and it is the Orthodox tradition that connects that country with other Eastern European countries. (It is the experience of long rule by the Ottomans which, in another sense, connects it to the Balkans.) Kievan Rus, centred in modern Ukraine, was also influenced by the Byzantine tradition, but, after the fall of Byzantium, it was Russia which took over the role of the centre of the Orthodox world. Moscow became the 'third Rome' and, with its rising military strength, Russia became the ultimate regional power even in areas where Byzantium never managed to establish itself – in Eastern Europe proper. Today, these historical developments continue to inspire President Putin in his claims over Ukraine.

It was thus Russia which, by a twist of history and with the help of Orthodox Christianity, gradually became synonymous with Eastern Europe. This happened despite the fact that, for centuries, Russian influence did not reach further west beyond Ukraine and Poland and that, before World War II and its aftermath, Russians never ventured into Central Europe.

All this had political and social consequences for Eastern Europe proper, such as the late abolition of serfdom in the region. Also, the Orthodox tradition was primarily concerned with the heavenly and holy and much less with the affairs of this world. This too led to a growing gap in economic and social development between Central Europe and Eastern Europe proper.

Natural conditions made things even worse: east of Central Europe lay large swathes of sparsely inhabited lands. In contrast, in Western Europe, at the height of the Middle Ages, farming became very intensive (to keep up with the increasing demands of the densely populated areas of Western Europe) but there was little need for such intensification in 'Eastern Europe proper'. In fact, even the gap between Western Europe and Central Europe is often explained by the fact that the West was increasingly turning to more sophisticated forms of agriculture (dairy and meat), as well as to non-agricultural economic activities, resulting in Central Europe becoming the granary of Western Europe. (Today, Ukraine and Russia are the granaries of a good part of the world, as the war in Ukraine has so clearly revealed.) Because of its proximity, it could still successfully manage to export and transport agricultural products to the West which – until the arrival of the railway – was not possible or viable for countries lying further to the East. To get going, 'Eastern Europe proper' lacked both an economic stimulant that was physically near enough and a philosophic ambition within its own culture. In the absence of both, it began drifting away from Central Europe, and also, of course, from its cultural roots in the south-east where the Ottomans now ruled.

I have already mentioned the growing economic gap between Eastern and Western Europe from the year 1000 and, in particular, from 1500 onwards. We have no estimates for individual Eastern European countries for that period. For the year 1600, the average GDP in Eastern Europe is estimated at 548 dollars, while that of Austria was already 837 dollars. The lands on the territory of modern Netherlands had nearly doubled their income since 1500 to 1,381 dollars, the highest in Europe, while that of the modern-day UK was 974. What today are Greece and Finland remained below the Eastern Europe average, but Spain and Portugal took off, largely because of the discoveries in the New World. A hundred years later, in 1700, the Eastern European average GDP per capita is estimated at 606 dollars. That of the UK was then almost double that figure (1,250) and the Netherlands had got an even firmer lead with 2,130 dollars. Greece and Finland, each at its own fringe of Europe, were again lagging behind or were just about catching up with the Eastern European average.[20]

To summarise this episode of Eastern European history, over the centuries, things turned upside down in the region. In the early Middle Ages, Greek Byzantium stood a good chance of becoming the master even in Central Europe. Greek missionaries, most notably Constantine and Methodius, operated among the early Czechs, Slovaks and Slovenians but were ultimately evicted and replaced by German and (for a short period) more amicable Irish missionaries. Thus these lands were already lost to Byzantium and Orthodox Christianity at a very early stage of history. The schism in the Church created the gap between Central and Eastern Europe. The gap between Central Europe and the Balkans, however, was created and then cemented by the Ottoman conquest. Greece, once the pivot of Europe and later of Eastern Europe and Orthodox Christianity, lost its primacy of the East and even of Orthodox Christianity. Such was the extent of this loss that today we are not accustomed to think of Greece as an Eastern European (and Balkan) country at all. In another

---

20. All data is from Maddison.

twist of history, after its accession to the EU, Greece began to feature in the popular mind as a Western European country. In a way, the job of those medieval barbarians from the West had been completed.

Islam Creates the Balkans

With the Ottoman conquest of Byzantium (Constantinople) in 1453, the lands that once marked the dividing line between the Western and Eastern Roman Empires and later between the Franks and the Greeks were turned into a buffer zone between the Ottoman Empire and the Holy Roman Empire. Although at one point the Ottomans made it as far as Vienna, they never permanently settled west of this East-West divide. The fall of Constantinople as the capital of an already fading Eastern Empire seemed to make it easy for the Ottomans to conquer the rest of that empire. On the other hand, Western Europe pulled itself together to establish a more coordinated and effective defence against the Ottomans and did not allow them to progress further west.

Europe, as shaped by the Ottoman invasion, then remained almost the same until the nineteenth century. The establishment of 'Turkey in Europe', as the Ottoman-occupied zones were known and, on the other side of the divide, the rise of the Habsburg Empire in Central Europe, effectively separated Eastern Europe into three tiers:

• The Balkans (south-east Europe) which was occupied by the Turks and consisted of modern-day Greece, Bulgaria, Serbia, Montenegro, Bosnia, Albania, North Macedonia,

parts of Romania and parts of what was then Hungary
- Central Europe and the Baltic shores (i.e. Eastern Europeans within the Habsburg or German Empire) which consisted of the modern-day Czech Republic, Poland, Slovakia, Slovenia, Hungary, the shores of the Baltic states, parts of modern day Romania and most of Croatia
- Eastern Europe 'proper' (i.e. the part of Eastern Europe that remained under the more or less strong influence of Russia and is largely Orthodox) which was made up of modern-day Belarus, Ukraine, parts of Poland, Romania, Moldova and parts of the Baltics.

As we can see, there was (and still is today) a degree of overlap. Parts of Poland and the Baltic states, though generally Catholic or Protestant, also experienced some influence from Russian Orthodoxy. Further south, the Balkans shared both the Orthodox Christian tradition and the experience of the Ottoman occupation but the Ottomans also occupied parts of Catholic Hungary, Croatia and Bosnia. (The reason why Medjugorje, the world-famous pilgrim site in the ethnic-Croatian part of Bosnia and Herzegovina, called Herzegovina, is managed by the Franciscan order is that they were the only Catholic clergy allowed to operate by the Ottomans.) As a result, the Balkans is where the Western (Catholic), Eastern-Orthodox and Oriental-Muslim traditions meet. They form the true multicultural region of Europe and they were like that long before modern Turks, Moroccans, Algerians and other Muslims set foot in Western Europe. They are the true and probably only true home of European Islam – something we should not forget when talking about integrating Muslim immigrants into European society.

Another important thing to note about the Balkans is that, while the concept of 'Eastern Europe' includes Central Europe and 'Eastern Europe proper', the war in former Yugoslavia has resulted in the Balkans somehow being excluded from it. Indeed, in the late 1980s and early 1990s, Yugoslavia was rarely mentioned in the context of democratic transition, but almost exclusively with relation to the war there, which many saw as a civil and ethnic strife. The rise of Serbian nationalism under Milošević (with some help from the Croatian nationalism of Franjo Tudjman, although the two cannot be compared exactly) resulted in the somewhat surprising fact that Yugoslavia, once the most progressive part of the former Communist world, began to lag seriously behind the rest of the Communist world in terms of democratic development. More than thirty years later this still has practical consequences in terms of the delay on their way to the EU too.

Not only Milošević but also the Serbian Academy of Science and the overwhelming majority of the Serbian public entirely missed the point about what was happening in the late 1980s. While rightly concerned that Yugoslavia was going to fall apart and fearing that this would eventually result in ethnic communities of Serbs scattered across Yugoslavia and no longer living in one single state (something that the Serbs had achieved with the creation of the Yugoslav Kingdom at the end of World War I), they decided to prevent that by the use of the (federal) army over which they had control. It was a tragic mistake for everyone in Yugoslavia but – strategically speaking – it was worst of all for the Serbs. (What would have happened had the Serbs, instead of opting for violent nationalism, put themselves at the front of an all-Yugoslav, genuinely democratic movement which favoured federalism, thus preserving Yugoslavia?) They paid a high price and, until after the fall of Milošević, they were excluded from the European Union's plans for the Balkans, being overtaken by Bosnia and Herzegovina, North Macedonia and Montenegro. This past mistake continues to trouble Serbia, as does its – almost exclusively emotional – attachment to Russia. Well, sometimes it pays off when it comes to gas.

Only after arms were finally laid down with the NATO intervention in Serbia and Kosovo in 1999, and United Nations administration was imposed in Kosovo the very same year, were efforts begun on the side of the Balkan nations and Brussels to allow them gradually back into the political realm of Eastern Europe by putting them on the EU track.[21] More than 20 years later the process is more or less at the beginning, due to both lack of inner capacities of the countries concerned and absence of true enthusiasm on the part of the Western European electorate, in particular in France and the Netherlands.

But let's return to the fifteenth century! While the Balkans were being conquered by the Ottomans, the Central European part of Eastern Europe, through its early adoption of Western Christianity and through its contact with the Germanic world, managed to maintain its inclusion in the Western world. It enjoyed relative political stability and the vicinity of the economic axis of Europe. Nations further east were at a lower socio-economic stage of development (for reasons explained earlier), while nations under Ottoman rule lost contact with mainstream Europe to a high degree.

---

21. Serbs find it difficult to comprehend that Bulgaria and Romania, for example, are already EU members, but they are not (yet). From the point of view of the general level of development, the feelings of the Serbs are justified. In 1990, before the war started in former Yugoslavia, the GDP of what was then Serbia/Montenegro was USD 5,249. In the same year, the GDP of Bulgaria was USD 5,597 and that of Romania USD 3,511. Figures are from Maddison, p. 101 and 105. To this purely economic comparison one should add the fact that, after World War II, Serbia was much more open to the West than the other two countries, at least in terms of the flow of ideas and the ability to travel freely to the West.

The Ottoman era in Europe is also the time when the term 'Eastern Europe' was coined. According to Wolff,[22] the modern concept of Eastern Europe originates in the attempts of eighteenth-century philosophers to find a physical location for the state of mind they considered opposite to that of the Enlightenment. Although they believed so deeply in the importance of reasoning and empirical evidence, the key figures in this process, Voltaire and Rousseau, seem never to have actually visited Eastern Europe. Further handicapped by the embryonic state of the geographical and linguistic sciences of the time, their accounts suggested a place of uniform and unvarying poverty, backwardness, ruthlessness and dullness – a vision that has in large measure persisted until the present. It was only the rise of a number of independent states in Central and Eastern Europe after World War I that, as we will see in Chapter 6, began to change this picture. Unfortunately, Yalta and the Iron Curtain cemented this view for another 50 years.

Western writers during the period of Ottoman rule in south-east Europe found a particular satisfaction in their discovery of these lands, either in reality (by means of travel) or in imagination. 'Eastern Europe' in those times could mean the Ottoman-occupied lands of south-east Europe or what I have called 'Eastern Europe proper'. There was not a clear definition, nor was there a need for one. The Oriental elements of the Ottoman Empire inspired as much fear as fascination, and both feelings informed views of the countries beyond the 'Iron Curtain' of the time. Facts about these countries did not really matter as much as the imagination. The alleged ferocity of the bloodthirsty Ottomans, which began to be associated with the lands beyond the Curtain, somehow impressed the

---

22. See *Inventing Eastern Europe* in the Bibliography.

Western world. The Dracula character stems from this source. In modern times it has been revisited by comparable works of fiction. A similar contemporary stereotype was created by Hollywood in the 2005 film *Hostel* in which two naïve American students, seeking sex and drugs, end up in a torture chamber in Slovakia. Stereotypes can be reinforced by movies from Eastern Europe itself. After the screening in a Dutch cinema of a Bosnian movie about the dilemmas of a group of desperate and lonely women in a remote village, a Bosnian lady said to me: 'This is the picture the people of Western Europe want to have about us: poor and nice. It is a strange sort of comfort for a Dutchman leaving the cinema and thinking, "Thank God I am not Bosnian! We may be in the midst of a global financial crisis but I will be looked after; my comfortable life as a European citizen will not be disrupted that greatly. I will not be left to my own destiny and to the elements somewhere up in the Bosnian hills with no future to look forward to".'

The fall of the Berlin Wall revived the fascination of the Western world with the East, in a mixture of disdain, naivety, envy and self-indulgence. The poverty of the East has been a confirmation of Western high standards of living and the idealised primordial warmth of the East, a nostalgic reminder of social conditions it has long lost.

Fast forward two and a half decades later, the reactions of Central European EU member states to the migration crisis and the rise of social conservatism in Poland, Hungary and elsewhere changed that cosily patronising attitude, itself a source of frustration in Eastern Europe. Fascination was gone, replaced by bewilderment and rejection, and even regret for having accepted these countries into the EU. As a result, there is little chance that the Western Balkans hopefuls will be seen in a better light by the electorate in France and the Netherlands.

The European Commission now regards the Western Balkans (the simple term 'Balkans' is apparently too discredited) as the following countries: Albania, Bosnia and Herzegovina, Kosovo, North Macedonia, Montenegro and Serbia. Romania, Bulgaria (the home of the actual Balkan Mountains) Croatia and even Greece were excluded. Apparently, the Balkans is not a geographic or historic term, but a political one, a state of mind, and inclusion or exclusion from this concept depends on political circumstances, such as membership of the European Union. It is an emotionally, or perhaps even ideologically, charged term. Naturally, such a view does not encourage anyone to stay in the Balkans long. But at least until Slovenia's entry into the European Union, attempts by Slovenians to disassociate the country from the (alleged) negative attributes of the Balkans have usually been met by derision: the Eastern Europeans themselves are not to have their own East or South.[23]

The name 'Balkans' actually comes from a mountain chain in southern Bulgaria, on the border with Greece. (This is why the Bulgarian national airline used to be called Balkan Airlines before it closed down in 2002.) To the Bulgarians,

---

23. There is a similar issue in the Baltic states, which prefer to consider themselves Nordic, like the Swedes or the Finns. It is Western Europeans who feel they can, for the sake of simplification, call Estonians Baltic and not Nordic, simply because it is somehow assumed that a former Communist country cannot be placed in the same group as 'fancy' countries like Sweden. The three Baltic countries now take some satisfaction in Nordic-Baltic cooperation (visible, for example, by their embassies abroad jointly celebrating National Days) and by presenting a common stance on EU financial matters through an informal grouping called the New Hanseatic League – a Nordic-Baltic version of Višegrad, mimicking the historic trade alliance in Europe's North.

their Balkan heights are what the Alps are to the Swiss and other Alpine nations, and they are none too happy to see other nations in the region being described as Balkan. The fact that the Balkan Mountains actually lie in Bulgaria probably led diplomats to rebrand the region as the Western Balkans, although geographically this makes little sense. Where are the Eastern Balkans then? And what exactly makes the Western Balkans different from the Eastern Balkans? Where does the peninsula end and the mainland begin in the case of the Balkans? For some, the Balkans begins in Trieste/Trst; for others it is already present in Munich or at Vienna *Südbahnhof* railway station – anywhere where people from the Balkans can be seen in numbers.

Historically, the Balkans means the area of south-east Europe that used to be under Ottoman rule. (It was once also a way of naming Europe, as seen from Ottoman Istanbul and, before that, from Byzantine Constantinople.) The loss of the Balkans was a terrible blow to the Turks and, in some quarters of Turkey, it is a matter for grief and regret even today. Modern Turkey sees itself as a player in the region. It is an important investor and a political force sympathetic to the region's development, and caring for the situation of its Muslim population. But with President Erdoğan's policies at home and abroad, many in the West have some worries about Turkish influence in the Western Balkans too.

The Turkish perspective on the history of the region (and, by extrapolation, to some extent also on its present and future) is, naturally, quite different from that of the Greeks and the Slavic nations of south-east Europe. For the Turks, these nations stabbed the Ottoman Empire in the back, after it had provided for centuries a stability and a peace that the region had not previously enjoyed – a view that is not entirely without substance.

Some Turks concluded that the key mistake that led to the loss of the Balkans was made with the decision not to force the Muslim religion upon the subject people,[24] which would also confirm the view that the Orthodox Church needs to be credited for the survival of the Balkan nations. In Bosnia, on the other hand, the lack of a comparably strong Church organisation and the presence of a distinctive Christian sect called Bogomilism, with some theological features close to Islam, made conversion easier. Essentially, though, accepting Islam under Ottoman rule meant, above all, an opportunity to climb up the social ladder of Bosnia at the time. Still, only a relatively small part of the Balkans actually converted to Islam and these peoples were seen by their Orthodox neighbours simply as 'Turks' until very recently. (This is where the historical roots for the dislike between the Serbs and the Albanians in Kosovo or the Serbs and the Muslims in Bosnia lie.) Today, Islamic Eastern Europe includes Albania, Kosovo, parts of North Macedonia and Bosnia – places that are usually associated with ethnic conflicts and/or war. But very few people in the West realise that these are actually the only European countries with an indigenous Muslim population. It is *the* centre of European Islam, much more so than the UK, France or Germany where Muslim populations are the product of much more recent immigration from non-European countries. In addition, Bosnia, long before the war started, had a historic record of genuine religious tolerance and a tradition of secular Islam. In many respects, secular Bosnian Islam was actually the main building element in the

24. See Tanil Bora, *Turkish national identity, Turkish nationalism and the Balkan problem* in *the Balkans: A Mirror of the New International Order*, Günay Göksu Özdoğan and Kemâli Saybaşih (eds.), Marmara University, 1995.

country that today we call Bosnia and Herzegovina – a fact that the local ethnic Serbs and also Croats do not much like to hear. While some may have doubts whether Turkey lies in Europe, there is certainly no doubt about the position of Bosnia.

For some time, the country has been trying very hard (but perhaps not hard enough) to reach an agreement between the Serbs, the Bosniaks and the Croats over future constitutional arrangements. The EU even went so far as to bend slightly what were originally very tough criteria, which led the country to sign the Stabilisation and Association Agreement in June 2008 – something that was met with great joy all over Bosnia and Herzegovina. But the momentum was soon lost and the EU and the US continue to be concerned that the ethnically almost purified Republika Srpska will simply go its own way, uninterested in doing business with the Muslim-Croat part of the country, where many Croats too look more to Zagreb than Sarajevo.

But imagine what a more sensible approach by the Serbs, Croats and Muslims alike could do for the country, making it, at some point in the future, the first EU member state with a sizeable indigenous Muslim population. In an era of tense relations between the Western (nominally Christian) world and the Muslim world, this could be an added value for the European Union. When the EU candidate status was granted to Ukraine and Moldova in June 2022, some of the Central European countries called for Bosnia and Herzegovina to be treated the same, simply to end the internal deadlock in the country, but most of the EU-27 remain unconvinced – and Bosnia and Herzegovina had to wait a few more months before the European Commission proposed a candidate status for the country in October 2022.

Further south-east, Albania, which is also traditionally a Muslim country, is making an enormous effort to shake off the legacy of its brutal Communist past. It has a long way to go, although, by entering NATO in 2009, it made a great leap forward. Its neighbour and cousin, Kosovo, the sanctuary of Orthodox Serbia, finally got its long-awaited independence in 2008. No one saw it as an ideal solution. But in the end most governments in the West realised that an undefined status for Kosovo presented a greater risk for itself and the region than an independent Kosovo did for the stability of Serbia, despite being a truly difficult loss. (A loss that could have probably been prevented even after the fall of Milošević, had the assassination of Prime Minister Djindjić in 2003 not set the clocks back.) On the other hand, it is true that Serbia did not really want Kosovo, at least not in its entirety – it only wanted the territory, together with its Serbs and the Serbian heritage, but not its ethnic Albanians. It is now up to young Kosovo to figure out how the two ethnic communities can live together. Poverty, social conservatism, corruption, large-scale emigration and links to organised crime continue to be serious issues not only for Kosovo itself but also for other European countries such as Switzerland, France and Slovenia where (Kosovo) Albanians live in considerable numbers. (The UK has its own issue with the emigrants from Albania proper.) So far it appears that Kosovo has not yet used its potential compared with the rest of the ethnic Albanian population of the region.

Kosovo is not the only nation to have fled Serbia. Even the Serbians' Montenegrin half-brothers went their own way in 2006, fed up with the eternal struggle in Serbia between liberal pro-Europeanism and the various incarnations of post-Milošević nationalism, combined with flirting with Russia, which an important part of the electorate finds attractive. As of 2022 a similar battle within Montenegro is not yet decided.

Another neighbour of Kosovo, once simply Macedonia, now North Macedonia, is also a vulnerable part of the Balkans. The wounds of the relatively short inter-ethnic conflict between Albanians and Macedonians in 2001 have been largely healed and the saga with Greece over the use of the name 'Macedonia' resolved. Greece had felt that its poor and weak western neighbour had stolen the name. The Macedonians had been stubborn and had not wanted to give it up, even if EU and NATO membership were at stake. (Greece had effectively blocked the entry of the then former Yugoslav Republic of Macedonia into NATO at the organisation's summit in Bucharest in April 2008.) Indeed, they had not been helpful at all: to make a point they had named the country's main airport after Alexander the Great and had furbished the Prime Minister's office in Skopje with locally excavated artefacts from Greek times rather than those of early Slavic Christianity in the area, which would be more characteristically Macedonian. Some had gone as far as claiming that they are descendants of the ancient Macedonians, a claim which had made the Greeks furious. Now, it is very likely that some of the DNA of ancient Macedonians (ethnically different from but culturally very similar to the Hellenic-Greeks) is in the veins of the contemporary (North) Macedonians, but they share most of it with the Slavs who arrived in these parts almost a thousand years later. And it is here that one should look for the real causes of the bickering: northern parts of Greece are still populated by the remnants of a Slavic (Macedonian) population and their modest claims for a kind of minority status seem to threaten the sense of national unity that Greece has developed since World War I. In addition, this same population stood firmly on the Communist side in the Greek civil war in the late 1940s, which was certainly not helpful during the military regime and in the context of relations with Yugoslavia.

At last both nations came to their senses and found the strength to overcome respective sensitivities, signing the Prespa agreement in 2018. This paved the way to North Macedonia's membership of NATO in 2020. However, the road to the EU was then blocked by another neighbour, Bulgaria, which does not have a problem with the name, but – given their interwoven history and the close proximity of the two languages – questions the very existence of a separate Macedonian identity and language.

At the centre of the dispute between North Macedonia and Bulgaria are the formative years of both nations in the late nineteenth century, when the Ottoman Empire began to collapse and a number of south-eastern European countries formed or restored their autonomy, inspired by humanistic and Enlightenment ideals which had taken so much longer to arrive in the region.[25] Through the two so-called Balkan wars on the eve of World War I, Greece, Serbia, Bulgaria and Romania fully regained their independence, but what are now Macedonians got caught between Bulgaria, Serbia and Greece. After World War I, the new Kingdom of Yugoslavia, in reality an extension of the restored Serbian monarchy, took over most of the Balkan Peninsula, including Macedonians, then essentially treated as Serbs.

---

25. It is interesting to note how the Enlightenment ideals clashed with the Byzantine legacy – at least that was how the Greeks of the day saw this legacy. Averil Cameron writes in *The Byzantines*: 'Against the Enlightenment ideas with which the idea of Greek independence had been invested Byzantium seemed to belong to a tradition of darkness and medievaldom, and to be dangerously associated, especially through the Church, with Ottoman rule...' (p. 177).

In Bulgaria of today, however, there is a strongly-held view that (North) Macedonians are in fact Bulgarians, who by reasons of history and politics ended up in a nation state of their own. In 2022, the Bulgarian parliament finally showed readiness to give up its veto on the start of EU accession negotiations with North Macedonia, under a deal brokered by France, which was only accepted by the North Macedonian parliament with considerable pain. The good news was that this enabled both North Macedonia and Albania to make a step forward on what will nevertheless be a very long journey towards joining the EU.

At the time of greater enthusiasm for EU enlargement in the early 1990s, Western politicians probably genuinely believed that a big-bang enlargement would impress the public in the West (or perhaps upset people less?). Quite the reverse happened: the sheer scale of the enlargement caused fear among the citizens of EU-15 in an already insecure world of fierce global competition, sluggish economic growth and terrorism. Voters in France and the Netherlands confirmed this in their referenda on the Constitution. In 2006, the Commission openly took the view that further enlargement would have to be put on hold, and it began to apply the criterion of 'integration capacity' which is, in reality, the controversial 'absorption capacity' in a new guise. The fact is that, after 1990, politicians failed to produce a genuinely positive vision of a united Europe and to inform their electorates about the added value of new member states; too many have seen these new states as liabilities. Pressure from sceptical EU countries has only been increasing. Thus in 2020, on the initiative of President Macron, the European Union adopted a revised enlargement methodology, putting more focus on conditions of particular concern (above all the rule of law – a topic that we return to in the second part of the book), a greater role for member states in the process, streamlining of the enlargement process, and, as they promised, more predictability.[26] But none of this sufficed and in 2022 Macron called for a 'European political community',[27] which many understood as delaying the eventual EU membership of not only Ukraine (and Moldova and Georgia), but of Western Balkans hopefuls as well. The new initiative had its official launch in Prague in October 2022, attracting even the participation of post-Brexit UK, with further meetings announced to take place in Moldova, Spain and the UK. We still have to see what will this new initiative actually mean for the Western Balkans.

The new (economic) nationalism, born in Europe after the failure of the European Constitution and further encouraged by the financial crisis of 2008, preceded by the mixed experience of the opening of the labour market for workers from the new member states, seems to be taking its toll. To these one should add the protracted political and legal battles over the issue of freedom of movement of services (notably haulage) and over the payment of social benefits to family members of EU expat workers not residing with the working person, where Austria took the lead (and had in 2022 to accept a defeat after a long legal wrangling). And, after all, there is near total agreement that the perception of Eastern European workers in the UK greatly contributed to Brexit or was badly misrepresented by those in favour of Brexit.

The Western Balkans became the main victims of this enlargement fatigue, which, as it now seems, can only be healed with the geopolitical argument: the concern about

26. https://ec.europa.eu/commission/presscorner/detail/en/IP_20_181
27. https://www.france24.com/en/europe/20220509-macron-calls-for-european-political-community-that-could-include-ukraine-uk

the rise of authoritarian Russia and China, which have been making inroads into the Western Balkans too. Think, for example, of the failed project of the Chinese-built motorway in Montenegro that put the country on the verge of a default.[28] This argument was further strengthened by the case of Ukraine, but here the EU acted in a bold way and granted the victim of the Russian attack a candidate status in June of 2022. The truth is that reunification of the continent through enlargement of the EU – if sold to the public with political vision and courage – represents the best future that Europe could have and the only one that can give it lasting security.

As for World War I, its victors denied Austria-Hungary its ambitions to expand further south-east, but allowed Serbia to extend its influence further north-west. The Germanic drive towards the Adriatic was halted, but not everyone was happy or too hopeful about the prospects of the new Yugoslav state either. I will look at this period of restoration and relative prosperity in the Balkans and the wider Eastern Europe in the subsequent chapter. Before that I wish to look more closely at why Germany and Austria, once the two key players in Eastern Europe and the main actors in two world wars, lost their position of influence, and how that affected Eastern Europe.

---

28. https://www.reuters.com/article/montenegro-china-road-idUSL5N2 NC2VZ

The Germans and Central Europe

In the previous chapters we saw how the popular mindset tends to associate Eastern Europe with the unknown and the traditional. In some instances, however, the perceived 'backwardness' is seen in what seems a more positive light – as a demonstration of appreciation for the past. Indeed, Eastern Europe is sometimes seen or portrayed as a living folk museum, where antique objects, customs and old-fashioned people can be observed, but also where traditions used to provide the only aesthetic luxuries in the otherwise grim life of the Communist past.

Such an unwanted picture of Eastern Europe is at the centre of *Molvania*[29] – a book that appeared in 2003, in which odd Eastern European customs feature prominently. (Some bookshops put it among the travel books and some among the humour.) It was designed to look like a standard guidebook with details about history, national parks, beaches, where to go, where to stay and where to eat. The only problem is that it was about an invented, stereotypical Eastern European country named Molvania – an Eastern European version of Borat's Kazakhstan. Of course, the shabbiness, ugliness, dullness, backwardness and poverty of the place are emphasised to the

---

29. https://en.wikipedia.org/wiki/Molvan%C3%AEa

point of absurdity but the book is perhaps not so obviously humorous that some people will not start searching for Molvania on the map! It apparently looked more than just a parody, as the then UK Minister Keith Vaz is reported to have criticised it as exploiting prejudices.[30] *Molvania* was not the first attempt of its kind, though. In *Why Come to Slaka?* by Malcom Bradbury, first published in the 1980s, Slaka was the name (echoing Slav?) of another invented Eastern European country that was held up to ridicule.

In any event, Central Europe is indeed marked by common heritage features. The countryside of the Czech Republic, Austria, Slovenia etc. is dotted with signs of popular piety, such as small roadside chapels and wooden crucifixions in the fields, witnesses of a common Catholic tradition that unites the region.[31] Common features exist in cuisine and in artisan activity, as well as in folk music.

In this part of Eastern Europe, it was the Germanic influence that was the most important and was responsible for some of these shared traditions. The Germanic encounter with Eastern Europeans began as early as the times of the Franks, continuing throughout the centuries of the Holy Roman Empire of the German Nation and the Austrian Habsburg Empire right up to the Nazi period. It was German speakers who pushed the Slavs towards the east and the south, colonising the more sparsely populated areas and bringing with them also urban culture, advanced agricultural techniques and industry. This colonisation was organised but it did not yet have the characteristics of planned Germanisation. Whether the peasants were Slav or German did not make much difference

---

30. http://news.bbc.co.uk/2/hi/europe/3592753.stm
31. Fichtner, p. 145.

to the feudal lords, most of whom (though not all) were German-speaking. Still, the net effect was that the Germanic-Slavic ethnic border was pushed further to the east and to the south. So, for example, in Carinthia, the southern province of Austria, which in the early Middle Ages was the political centre of the early Slovenians, there is now only a minority Slovenian community.

Gradually, this silent change of the ethnic structure began to have political implications, as Germanic nobility took lands away from indigenous landlords, usually of local ethnic origin. In the nineteenth century, in the era of revolutions and the births of nation states, this became a serious issue. The relatively peaceful coexistence of Slavs and Germans began to collapse, destroying the Central European idyll. Slavic nations within the Austrian Empire began to fight for their place in the sun. Usually the battle took the peaceful form of vigorous political and civil campaigns for the public use of the local Slavic language and enforcement of already existing legislation in favour of equality. There was pressure to change the signage on public offices, pubs and shops. There were colourful political confrontations on urban and provincial councils, and there was competition between rival societies and social clubs, sport organisations, etc. However, clashes between protesters and police occurred and there were even casualties. The fight was mostly fought in the cities, because it was there that most German speakers resided. Sometimes they even formed a majority of the urban population, surrounded by an almost exclusively Slavic countryside.

The term 'Central Europe' (sometimes the German name *Mitteleuropa* is used) came into existence during the process of German nation-building. It was a Prussian invention, which was then taken over by the Habsburgs and later also by the

Visegrad countries (Poland, the Czech Republic, Slovakia and Hungary) and has been used right up to the present day. Nineteenth-century debates about German identity and the future of the nation focused around the issue of securing the resources needed for the economic development of the German Empire. While colonies were considered as an option, many Germans thought that Germany should, above all, build a wider sphere of influence for itself, both economic and political, in its immediate neighbourhood. Although these ideas were also used by extreme nationalists and ultimately degenerated into an excuse for the Nazi conquest of Europe, their origins were more benign. One of the best-known advocates of the creation of a Central Europe as a single economic and political area was Friedrich Naumann, an early twentieth-century, liberal member of the German parliament. Naumann's book with the same title (*Central Europe*[32]) advocated the creation of a loose, above all economic, European federation to include Germany, Austria-Hungary, Poland and countries further afield, from the Vistula river to the Vosges Mountains and from Galicia to Lake Constance, a 'welding together of the German Empire and the Austro-Hungarian Dual Monarchy'. The entity would use German as its main official language, but all the nations would be equal and would have the right to use their own vernaculars. Reading the book, one finds surprising similarities not only to the Eurojargon of the present EU but also to issues discussed today in relation to the European Constitution. For example, Naumann writes that issues of 'creed and nationalities' 'should not be subjected to any centralised regulation... nor will the super-State have anything to do with school affairs'. Similarly, the 'much disputed language question must be left

---

32. Published by Alfred A. Knopf, New York, 1917.

to the decision of the individual States', as should internal administration. He talks about some of the legislation being dealt with by a 'Mid-European Commission', housed in one place, with specialised offices in Frankfurt, Hamburg, Berlin, Vienna and Prague. The 'super-State' would be governed by a 'treaty system as the basis of Mid-European unity' and so on.

Naumann's idea, which some saw as essentially imperialistic, was buried in the ashes of two world wars (although a similar idea of an All-Danube federation resurfaced in the 1930s and 1940s among Eastern European intellectuals). It was, however, resurrected as an all-European idea in the project of the European Communities and later the European Union – two world wars were needed before Europe looked at this idea seriously.

World War I offered a number of Eastern European countries the opportunity to escape Germanic influence and regain independence. Poland was resurrected, and two new, rather artificial states were created: Czechoslovakia and Yugoslavia. Yet, during World War I, many Slovenians, Czechs, Slovaks and Poles fought as Austrian soldiers – a duty they must have performed with very mixed feelings. Austria was increasingly a bad mother to them, favouring its German-speaking children. But the prospect of, say, Russian rule for Polish people or Italian rule for Slovenians was not particularly inspiring either.[33] From that point of view, the creation of independent national or multinational Slavic states, however imperfect, was seen as probably the best possible outcome. In the end, World War I left Germany and Austria humiliated, reduced,

---

33. In Trieste/Trst region, the ambitions for Italian national unity found the local ethnic Slovenians on the Austrian side of the fence subjected to growing pressure, discrimination and, with the advent of Fascism, outright persecution.

and perhaps, as German-speaking subjects themselves felt, misunderstood. Austrians in particular felt that they had been betrayed by the Slavs, and they did not recover for some time. The feeling of loss is not completely gone even today. In a private discussion about Kosovo in 2007, a high-ranking Austrian diplomat remarked to an embittered Serbian minister that Austria too had had to go through the process of losing part of its territory. After World War I that was certainly also the feeling of Slovenians, as Slovenian-populated south Carinthia ended up in the newly formed Republic of Austria.

But it was World War II which has had an even more dramatic and decisive impact on the living memory of the peoples of Eastern Europe. In that war, Slavs were second only to Jews in the list of those for whom the Nazis had a murderous contempt.[34] They were also second only to Jews in the numbers who fell victim to the Nazis. (In Yugoslavia, Albania and Greece, the troops of Fascist Italy also committed horrible crimes against civilian populations – a fact later obscured when the Italians switched allegiance in 1943.) This altered relationships in Eastern Europe dramatically, reducing the appeal of German culture and its role there. After World War I, Austria had to renounce its rule over large swathes of Eastern Europe and also its own idea of a Central Europe. By contrast, after World War II, Germans withdrew from Eastern Europe not only as defeated former occupying forces, but also culturally. After more than a thousand years of shared history,

---

34. 'The Nazis treated Western Europeans with some respect, if only the better to exploit them, and Western Europeans returned the compliment by doing relatively little to disrupt or oppose the German war effort. In Eastern and South-eastern Europe the occupying Germans were merciless, and not only because local partisans – in Greece, Yugoslavia and Ukraine especially – fought a relentless if hopeless battle against them.' See Tony Judt, *Postwar: A History of Europe since 1945,* William Heinemann, London, 2005, p. 17.

the Slavic and the Germanic worlds were finally separated. The Iron Curtain only reinforced this.

Local ethnic German populations in the Czech lands, in Poland, Slovenia and elsewhere were also often forced (or simply chose) to leave. Certainly the majority of these local ethnic Germans (although not all of them) had often been sympathetic to Hitler and the Nazis, and some were involved in war crimes too. Under special decrees by the then Czech President Beneš, almost all Czech Germans were forced to leave the country, leading to a bitterness that is still around today. It was at least partially alleviated by a solemn declaration made by Václav Havel and Helmut Kohl in 1992, addressing both the 1938 Munich Agreement which led to the annexation by Hitler of the areas of the Czech lands populated by ethnic Germans, and the forced expulsion of ethnic Germans from the same areas after World War II.[35] It took another quarter of a century for a joint committee of Czech and Austrian historians to produce a common account of the history of these two nations. But the mere fact that the two countries (perhaps even more so Austria) felt the need to commission such a report testifies to the depth of the Germanic-Slavic conflict and also of the importance of history in Central Europe.[36]

In Slovenia, there was not exactly a forced expulsion but the measures adopted against the 'sympathisers of the occupying forces' had a similar effect on a much smaller scale. Here, the situation was even more complicated. While most ethnic

35. For a detailed account of Czech-German relations in the nineteenth and twentieth centuries see Benes, Z et al, *Facing History – The evolution of Czech-German Relations in the Czech provinces, 1848–1948,* 2002 (published in English in the Czech Republic).
36. Šmidrkal, V, Konrad, U, Schmoller, H, Perzi, N, (eds.), *Sousedé. Česko-rakouské dějiny,* MUA 2019.

Germans were living in the urban centres of Yugoslavia before World War II, there was also the very special case of an ethnic-German community in south-east Slovenia, around the town of Kočevje. These so-called Kočevje (or Gottscheer) Germans were the remains of medieval German colonisation, a closely-knit community that preserved an archaic form of German. They had worked hard through centuries, clearing the woods to create a flourishing farming society which lived in a fairly harmonious relationship with the surrounding ethnic Slovenians until the advent of Nazism – Hitler's emissaries began to fuel unrest and pro-Nazi sentiment among them, promising their return to the original homeland. But, when World War II broke out, the Kočevje area fell into the Italian zone of occupation. So Hitler, in keeping with the promise, and Mussolini, eager to round up the territory, agreed to have them removed from their traditional homes and sent not to their medieval lands of origin in heartland Germany, but to places of the forcibly enlarged Third Reich from which local Slovenians had, only days before, been expelled and despatched to Germany, Serbia and elsewhere.

Once the Kočevje Germans had left, their villages were largely destroyed by the Italian army to prevent them from being used by the Communist resistance movement that had headquarters in the woods in the area. What remained of the houses and churches of Kočevje Germans after the Italians were gone was then finally destroyed by the Communist authorities after the war, clearing the area of any memory of the community including, above all, its religious monuments. Moreover, this battered-down area also became the killing fields for Slovenian and other Yugoslav anti-Communist troops after the war. Finally, it was turned into an off-limits area, where only hunting havens and nuclear-proof shelters for the Slovenian political elite were allowed to exist. The Kočevje Germans were not mentioned again until after 1990 (and nor were the massacres of anti-Communists). Only then was it possible to state that Slovenia was poorer without a community that by that time had been long scattered around the globe. It was too late: another precious link between Eastern Europe and ethnic Germans had been destroyed. Now the local museum dedicated to their memory and the books published about them stand in place of their overgrown villages, lost amidst the dense forests that surround them.

If that sounds nostalgic to some it is perhaps because people in Eastern Europe who can still see some merits in the old Austrian Empire, despite all its faults, are also today at great risk of being seen as naïve. The unspeakable suffering caused to Slav nations by the Nazis (including many Austrians) erased most of the good memories of the times of earlier Habsburg rule. Any claim today that a more restrained German nationalism and a decision to make Austria-Hungary a federal state with strong autonomy for the Slavic nations would have saved it and perhaps would have created a European model-state, is easily dismissed as pure and naive speculation. The world of Central Europe as it existed for several centuries is said to be finally lost in the ashes of World War II. Even the German language, which was the *lingua franca* of Central Europe for centuries, was replaced by English (as with Russian in Central Europe), a language that belongs to modern times and to the wider world but not to the region. Not only that: the general public both in German-speaking and Slavic countries has today almost completely lost its awareness of a shared history and of being a part of the same Central European culture. History, as taught under Communism, assisted greatly in this process: not only did we learn to dislike Germans because of what the Nazis did to our countries during World War II but also because they used to be our feudal lords.

This loss is particularly striking in the case of Czechs and Slovenians, who were most closely connected with Germany and/or Austria. (The latter, through both its name and its geographical position, could actually be claimed as an Eastern European country: Österreich means 'Eastern Kingdom' and, if you are travelling from Prague or Ljubljana, you have to head *east* if you want to get to Vienna.) Among the oldest Viennese families, there are those whose family names still sound Slavic even though they are written in a German form. And it would be difficult for Slovenians to find a nation that was closer to them, in its political history or even ethnogenesis, than Austria. (Because of centuries in which they had a common border with Hungarian-ruled Croats, Slovenians have had less political and even cultural interaction with their immediate Slavic neighbours who are otherwise closest to them in language.) Or as an American writer put it: 'The bulk of Slovenians... had become "Austrian" (though not German) in the twelfth and fourteenth centuries. Culturally, but not linguistically, they are Austrians and with a certain amount of exaggeration one might say that the central and east Austrians are the only Germanised Slovenes, and the Slovenes the only non-Germanised Austrians – a definition that both sides would find most displeasing.'[37] Not necessarily so. Long before the above words were written, Ivan Cankar, the greatest Slovenian writer and most outspoken socialist politician of his time, who vigorously advocated the political union of Slovenians and other neighbouring Slavs, said in a public speech in 1913: 'In the cultural, let alone the linguistic sense there does not

---

37. Von Kuehnelt-Leddihn, p. 261.

exist a Yugoslav question! Perhaps it did exist once, but it was resolved when the south Slav tribe split into four nations with four fully independent cultural lives. We are brothers in blood, cousins at least as far as the language is concerned; but in culture, as a result of several centuries of separate education, we are more alien to each other than is our Gorenjska Region farmer distant to a Tyrolian one or a winemaker from Gorica to one from Friuli.'

This 'nostalgia' for Central Europe got a real shape in the 1990s, when Poland, the Czech Republic, Slovakia and Hungary, the countries known as the Višegrad Four (after the town of Višegrad in Hungary where, in 1335, the kings of Bohemia, Hungary and Poland met), reclaimed the title of Central Europe and forged a Central European alliance – but this time without Austria. It was the intellectuals in these countries who helped to reinstate the concept as they had already attempted to do during the Communist era and here the contribution of Austrians was important, especially through various NGOs.

The political grouping of the Višegrad Four was meant to facilitate the path of these countries towards accession into the EU, though the philosophical underpinning of the idea (the restoration of Central Europe) was met with a very mixed reaction in Western Europe. In some instances, it was interpreted as an unnecessary attempt to change the reality of the East-West division or as a handy excuse to avoid the label 'Eastern' or even as laying claim to a (Western) European legacy that was not to be shared with Eastern Europeans. Apparently, the idea of Central Europe challenged deeply ingrained views of Eastern Europe as a region inherently different and distant from the West, perhaps even as a place that needs to exist in order to justify the existence of 'Western

Europe'. (Interestingly, doubts may have been expressed about the existence of a Central European identity but there never seem to be any doubts that an Eastern European identity exists.)

After their accession to the European Union the four countries continued their close collaboration on various EU policies, becoming a force to be reckoned with, above all in Brussels. However, in the 2010s, the group began to raise eyebrows there and in Western capitals with the increasingly socially conservative policies of some of the governments and with what was regarded as the violation of the rule of law principles in Poland and Hungary. This encouraged the now slightly uncomfortable Czech Republic and Slovakia to look for alternatives, for example, the Slavkov/Austerlitz format that connects the two countries with Austria. To the south, Slovenia that – mainly due to internal lack of consent – had failed to join the V4, in 2020 joined the Austrian idea of a C5 group, i.e. the V4 minus Poland plus Austria and Slovenia. But common interests, especially when it comes to EU funds, continue to prevail and the V4 still get together in Brussels whenever needed. Should the EU decide in the future to broaden the scope of the so-called Quality Majority Voting, the V4 and other groupings of Central European (and other) countries will only gain in importance.

For Slovenia, despite its close historical links to Austria, laying claim to Central European status was a more difficult task. Mostly because of the imagined baggage it brought from its years as part of Yugoslavia, above all the war in Yugoslavia, Slovenia also failed to earn membership in the Višegrad group which it desperately wanted at a certain time (although this was denied later by leftist governments) in order to speed up its approach to the EU and NATO and, above all, to decouple itself from the Balkans. In the end, Slovenia joined the EU at the same time as the Višegrad Four but they got NATO membership a few years earlier.

Most Slovenians had, as a matter of fact, left Central Europe at the end of World War I, when Slovenians, Croats and Serbs living within Austria-Hungary proclaimed the so-called State of the Slovenians, Croats and Serbs. This included modern-day Slovenia, Croatia, Bosnia and Herzegovina and the northern Serbian province of Vojvodina with its sizeable Hungarian population and other ethnic minorities. However, nobody wanted to recognise this state and the Italians, following a secret clause in the London Treaty that rewarded Italy for its change of sides, invaded most of what today is western Slovenia, including the village of Vrhpolje mentioned in the introductory chapter. In these circumstances, the young State of the Slovenians, Croats and Serbs was pressed to merge with the Kingdom of Serbia under the Serbian crown – something that Slovenians, let alone Croats, never really wanted. (Despite their pan-Slavic feelings for the Serbs, both Slovenes and Croats had been appalled by the assassination of the Austrian archduke in Sarajevo in 1914 by a Serbian nationalist.) Serbia and its king were very well aware that former Slav subjects of Austria had little leverage and rushed through the swiftly assembled parliament a Constitution that favoured Serbia. Suddenly, the Slovenians found themselves in the same state with lands and peoples that for centuries had been part of the former Ottoman Empire, and with which they only shared either distant Slavic roots or sometimes not even those. The only Central European Slovenians left were those in Austria, though they too were not rewarded for their loyalty to the new Austrian Republic but became subject of a new wave of Germanisation.

To understand the later conflicts within Yugoslavia, it is therefore important to note that Yugoslavia was not a natural choice for many of the peoples included in it – except for the Serbs, who saw it as an extension of their own kingdom. True, the Yugoslav (meaning 'south Slav') kingdom did provide for a temporary shelter from German nationalism. At the same time, Slovenians entered a new geopolitical context, the Balkans. There was little common history and memory to share, except pan-Slavic myths. Not surprisingly, therefore, the concept of the Yugoslav nation never really took off.

In foreign relations, the new kingdom was primarily concerned about its relations with the immediate neighbours of the Serbs, above all with Bulgaria. (There was even talk of a merger with Bulgaria.) There was not enough incentive left to deal with the territorial claims of Italy and Austria. Indeed, the western part of what is today Slovenia was after World War I swiftly occupied by Italy, while in the Slovenian-populated Carinthia (now a province in Austria) a plebiscite was held. There, the prospect of Serbian dominance convinced many ethnic Slovenians to opt for Austria. But after the area did become a part of the new republic, previous Austrian assurances of cultural autonomy for ethnic Slovenians in Carinthia were forgotten and, with the advent of Nazism, Slovenians there became its first target, but also Austria's foremost resistance. Despite that not even post-WW II Austria managed to respect minority rights in full. Successive regional Carinthian and federal Austrian governments failed to fulfil their international obligations, above all to codify the use of Slovenian language. In 1972, media, police and authorities stood idle watching nationalist mobs destroying bilingual road signs, erected in accordance with the Austrian State Treaty. Forty years later a constitutional act bypassed the Treaty, securing only a fraction of the original number of bilingual names of places. Although the atmosphere has improved now that communist Yugoslavia no longer exists, in Carinthia the minority still faces prejudices and an unwillingness to acknowledge it publicly. Interestingly this receives little attention in the European media, perhaps because such attitudes are difficult to reconcile with the otherwise positive international image of Austria. Chauvinists are usually sought elsewhere – in Eastern Europe. Not even a very noble apology, issued in Slovenian in 2020, a century after those events, by the President of Austria Mr Van der Bellen, has changed much.

Elsewhere, in relations with Italy, it was the Slovenian President Pahor and his Italian counterpart Mattarella who showed their courage. In 2020, on the centenary of the Fascist arson of the landmark Slovenian cultural centre in Triest/Trst, depicted later by the famous writer Boris Pahor (no relation to the President), they simultaneously laid flowers at the memorial to members of the Slovenian anti-fascist resistance executed in 1930 (formally still characterised by the Italian legal system as terrorists) and at the memorial to Italians (and other anti-Communists) massacred by Yugoslav partisans in the immediate aftermath of World War II, then thrown into natural caves, called *foibe* in Italian. Their gesture became an object of heavy criticism by both the radical left in Slovenia and some of Giorgia Meloni's loyalists in Italy. But in the big picture, it became evident that while the dismantling of Central Europe took two wars to be completed, it took even longer to make some (if not full) sense of the events that are the subject of the next chapter.

The Age of Totalitarianisms

In Ottoman-ruled south-east Europe, the nineteenth century was marked by uprisings against the Turkish overlords. Greeks started rebelling in 1821 and finally succeeded in gaining their independence a few years later. The liberation movement started in Bulgaria at about the same time. Nationhood was won in the late 1870s in at least part of the country but full independence was achieved only at the beginning of the twentieth century. The timeframe was similar for Serbia. The principalities of Wallachia and Moldavia were united under the name of Romania in the mid-nineteenth century. A modernisation of Romanian society, previously under Ottoman and Russian rule, commenced and full independence from the Ottomans was achieved in 1877. Indeed, this was a landmark year for all the countries of south-east Europe because of Russia's victory over the Ottoman Empire which helped them in their own fight for independence – something about which Russians will have reminded these nations even during the recent aggression against Ukraine a century and a half later.

In Central Europe too, as we saw earlier, the nineteenth century was a time of nationalist revival, echoing the general mood in the rest of Europe. Germany and Italy were created at much the same time – both are relatively young nation-states too! While in south-east Europe the national movements were directed against the Ottomans, in Central Europe the main adversaries were the Germans and the Austrians. A revolutionary spirit spread among the Slavic nations within the Austro-Hungarian Empire (and Prussia) and, as has already been mentioned in the previous chapter, a cultural struggle began. This struggle was also reflected in the arts of Eastern European countries of the time. As Stephen Mansbach has written, 'As a consequence of the nineteenth- and twentieth-century limitations on the free exercise of political, economic, and personal liberties in the regions of the Continent subject to Romanov, Hohenzollern, Habsburg, and Ottoman control, the visual arts assumed a primary responsibility as cultural custodian for the respective "subject nations". Hence, artists of these regions often elected to emphasise national individuality rather than universality. They responded variously to a public demand for expressions of national self-consciousness through which an emerging nation might stake its claim simultaneously to singularity and to membership in a modern world. Such profession of national identity through the medium of progressive art was a cultural phenomenon as widespread in Eastern Europe as it was rare in the west. Among the developed political states of Western Europe, modern national identity has been (and remains) the province of politicians and statesmen and only incidentally the concern of the artists; but then the nations of the West have often been free to express their identities politically.'[38]

---

38. SA Mansbach in *New Frontiers – Art from New EU Member States*, National Gallery of Ireland, 2004. Mansbach certainly has a point, and the poem to Napoleon and later his statue are good examples. But art *was* used for nationalist/political purposes in many of the Western countries too, though at different points in time. If nothing else, nation building was there forged through war memorials and statesmen's statues, above all after the two world wars. Alain De Botton (in *Art as Therapy*, Phaidon, 2015, p. 201

In parts of Central Europe, mostly Slovenian and Croat lands, this national revival was briefly interrupted but also encouraged by the short-lived French occupation in the form of the so-called Illyrian provinces. This five-year period encouraged the use of vernacular and helped spread the values of the French Revolution among the few intellectuals, though the local Slovenian population did not honour the occasional desecration of churches by individual French soldiers and certainly did not avail themselves of the civil marriage option introduced by the French. But the Enlightenment spirits unleashed by this transitory French episode were strong enough that Valentin Vodnik, a Slovenian Catholic priest (!) welcomed the French, as restorers of a Slavic entity, with a poem. A century later, in 1929, a monument to Napoleon – reportedly the only statue to the French statesman outside France – was unveiled in Ljubljana to honour the centenary of the Illyrian Provinces and to strengthen the then Yugoslav-French alliance.

With the French or without them, towards the end of the nineteenth century, the nationalist movements in Eastern Europe culminated in demands that the Slavic nations should at least have autonomy within the Austrian Empire. However, there was no general consensus as to how this was to be achieved; before the end of World War I, not all Slavs thought of fully independent states. Most hoped that a federal solution within the empire could be reached, others that the help of the Allies, including Russia,

---

– 208) points to the wider concept of 'political art', for example, works by Anselm Kiefer, trying to address the 'appalling tragedy of Germany in the late 1930s and early 1940s' or the wrapping of the Reichstag (the German Federal parliament in Berlin) by Christo and Jeanne-Claude in 1995. And in 1955 Nikolaus Pevsner found Englishness in 'chairs, bookshelves and door-handles'.

should be sought. Amongst German and Austrian politicians, a minority were sympathetic to the ideas of federalism but most were carried along on the tide of ethnic German nationalism. Austria (and Hungary) feared losing access to the Adriatic, and losing Bosnia to Serbia. Above all, Austrians were scared of an outright end to the empire, something that eventually happened perhaps precisely because of the way the crisis was handled before it developed into World War I.

The war made little sense to the nations of Eastern Europe. It was not their war, although, as it dragged on, they realised that it might represent an opportunity for their national aspirations. Some of the Eastern European nations were in quite a complex situation. While the Austrian-occupied part of Poland became the centre of the movement to restore the Polish state, part of the country was also under the rule of Russia, one of the Allies in the war. Some in the Polish national movement thought that they could somehow, perhaps by playing the Slavic card, achieve (limited) independence with the help of Russia. At the same time, many Western Allies thought that Russia should not be upset by the idea of a Polish state but that the Poles should be left in the Russian zone of influence. Things became more complicated for the Poles with the Communist revolution in Russia when Lenin went on to sign a separate truce with the Central Powers. (A few decades later, Stalin would do something similar with Hitler.) The Western Allies were also concerned that a social revolution might spread from Russia (something, as we shall see, would worry European powers for the entire interwar period), which is why an independent Polish state came to be seen as a welcome buffer zone.[39] In the Czech and the Slovak

---

39. Wandycz, pp. 180–200.

lands there was also a pro-Western and a pro-Russian strand within the national movement.

In the very last months of the war, Eastern European nations, one by one, proclaimed their independence from the Austro-Hungarian Empire (and from Prussia). They were encouraged by American involvement in the war and, above all, by President Wilson's Fourteen Points, the most important of which acknowledged the right of national self-determination. Although there were conflicting interpretations of what exactly President Wilson meant by this, it marked the beginning of the love-affair of Eastern Europe with America at a time when the 'old' Europe was not able to sort out its own problems.[40]

Sometimes only indirectly, Russia played an important and positive role in the independence struggle of a large number of Eastern European nations. (Although the Slovenians and the Croats, for example, were not really affected by Russia.) For a time it appeared that perhaps even the long-standing conflict with the Poles could be resolved. All this was suddenly brought

---

40. The right of nations for self-determination again resurfaced at the time of the break-up of Yugoslavia – another occasion when the Continent was unable to solve its own affairs and US involvement was needed – and then again with the issue of Kosovo. Do the people of Kosovo possess this right? The answer given by the International Court of Justice in The Hague was not straightforward. The Court merely stated that 'the declaration of independence of Kosovo, adopted on 17 February 2008 did not violate international law'. Indeed, many believe that it is not possible to give a straightforward answer because there seems to be no legal definition of what exactly constitutes a 'people', and the principle of self-determination is in conflict today with another principle of the inviolability of the territorial integrity of states. Interestingly enough, as many as 36 countries from across the globe sent their submissions to that question to the ICJ in the spring of 2009. The UK, in the case of Scotland, and Spain, in the case of Catalonia, approach this issue from different angles.

to a halt by the Soviet revolution and soon a rather sinister Soviet policy towards Eastern Europe emerged.

Elsewhere, the new Austrian republic built on the ruins of the Austrian Empire, humiliated and frustrated, shrank to little more than the German-speaking part of the former empire. The Slavic nationalisms of the nineteenth century created an image of the empire that, perhaps, it did not deserve, and it was this image that the triumphant new Eastern European nations were happy to abandon and venture enthusiastically into an unknown future on their own.

A look at the map of post-World War I Eastern Europe reveals a hugely reduced Hungary, an enlarged Romania, and an independent Albania, Bulgaria and Greece. On the shores of the Baltic Sea, Lithuania, Latvia and Estonia won independence from Tsarist Russia. After many years, Poland finally regained its independence. Two new states appear on the map as well: Czechoslovakia and Yugoslavia.

Yugoslavia and Czechoslovakia were a novelty, a product of Wilson's new principle of the self-determination of nations. They were an artificial attempt to create a nation by forming a state. This reflected the way in which many of the oldest European nations had been formed in the past, but with Czechoslovakia and Yugoslavia times had changed and things did not work out as planned – not even after 1990. These two countries (Yugoslavia even more so than Czechoslovakia) did not possess the common ethnicity, history and national myths which were needed to achieve homogenisation or cohesion in a new nation. At the time, Slovaks in Czechoslovakia and Slovenians and Croats in Yugoslavia realised that this was the best they could hope to achieve and that their quest for full national independence could not (yet) be successful. After all, the new states did represent protection against German and Hungarian (and to a lesser degree Italian) nationalism, which had been of major concern to the smaller nations for a very long time. The Czechoslovakian case was also well served by the charismatic figure of President Masaryk, a liberal politician ahead of his time.

Still, Europe in general looked quite promising in the 1920s. Unfortunately, the Communist revolution in Russia brought a new and previously unknown factor into the politics and society of Europe. Marxist academic ideas became flesh where they were least expected, in a country that had not yet become an industrial society. Vulgar Communism, as began to be practised in Soviet Russia, looked savage and totally alien to most people in the rest of Europe. For outsiders, it certainly added to their perceptions of the 'otherness' of Eastern Europe.

But it was not only about a fundamental change of governance *within* Russia itself. The new and quite unique feature was the Soviet ambition to transform the rest of Europe (and the world). That was the intention of the Soviet Communists from the very beginning: 'From the outset Communist parties were established across the globe and financed with vast sums of Russian money. [...] The customary forms of international relations were thus systematically overturned by Moscow's messianic commitment to overturning the established international order at all costs and as soon as practicable.' To that end, as early as 1919 the Soviets launched the Comintern, a semi-official agency tasked with coordinating Communist parties abroad and fomenting revolutions. So important was the export of the revolution to Lenin that he 'poured millions of dollars into the furthering of unrest worldwide – even while his own population in the south was driven to cannibalism in 1921.'[41]

---

41. Haslam, J, *The Spectre of War, International Communism and the Origins of World War II*, Princeton University Press 2021, pp. 5 – 6, 26.

There has been much debate as to why Communism took roots in Russia first. Some say that the Russian (and more generally the Slavic) soul is somehow more susceptible to collectivist ideas and that Russians were for ages used to the iron fist of their Tsars. Much as they detested it, so the argument goes, they also secretly admired it, and it was not difficult to have the Romanov Tsars replaced by a Communist Tsar – Stalin, or much later Putin. The alleged taste of the Orthodox Church for grandeur and for a strong nation-state is also supposed to fit into this picture – there another analogy can certainly be drawn with the Russian Orthodox Church's support for the war in Ukraine. There may also be some weight in the argument that a country as large and sparsely populated as Russia is difficult to govern, and therefore needs a strong centralist government. Anyway, Lenin was smart enough to realise that the utterly impoverished Russian peasantry (and the relatively few industrial workers in the country) would, at least initially, back any change. He also had the support of Germany, which saw benefit in anything that would make Russia weaker. Soon a monstrous totalitarian system was put in place, preceding its Fascist and Nazi counterparts that were soon to follow.

Indeed, the situation was not much different in the other two totalitarian systems of the interwar period that were produced by industrialised Western Europe during its worst ever economic crisis, the Great Depression. Nazism and Fascism had elements in common (and with Communism) but they came into existence in the very different social settings of Germany and Italy. The latter country was much poorer and its southern regions were, socially and economically, in a state of near feudalism. What was common to both was the attempt to solve the internal problems of a nation through military expansion, justified by a dangerous nationalistic or even racial ideology. Much more affluent than the Soviet subjects though the majority of them were, Germans and Italians also appeared susceptible to totalitarian ideas. There was something in these three political ideologies of the twentieth century that was radically different from the logic of any previous system of governance or any previous war for territory. Now it was about an ideology that encompassed all walks of life and all people, it was not just about power and land.

Initially, Hitler's and Mussolini's ideas were debated in perfectly respectable circles and had advocates all over Europe, even in democracies like Britain where Mosley's British Union of Fascists was formed. Members of the elites in Germany, Italy and elsewhere in Europe, who were fascinated by Fascism, dismissed its sinister character. 'The fact that fascism could gain political power in Italy and Germany was, to a great extent, a result of the hubris, as much as the cowardice and perfidy, of the social elites,' writes Rob Riemen, to provide parallels with populisms of the twenty-first century. 'The liberals no longer defended the freedom principle of European humanism...' Riemen makes a strong case for the argument that the rise of fascism and of mass-society in Europe then – a variant of pre-World War II populism[42] – was, above all, possible because of the loss of moral values.

In the beginning, some of the Fascist social and economic ideas were accepted as legitimate contributions to the debate about solving the deep problems of Europe at the time. The ultra-nationalistic and racial aspects of the two ideologies were apparently not taken seriously enough. After all, anti-Semitism – albeit not necessarily in its radical racist form – had long been

---

42. Riemen, R, *To Fight Against This Age: On Fascism and Humanism*, WW Norton & Company, 2018, pp. 55 – 56.

present in Europe, even in its most affluent parts, and needed only to be inflamed and developed further to result finally in the unspeakable horrors of the Holocaust.

As Haslam points out, 'throughout the 1930s leading Conservative politicians with the democracies not only welcomed fascism into power but thereafter also feared that, were fascism overthrown in Italy or Germany [...] communism would be almost certain to take its place.'[43] The communist menace was the number one consideration of European politicians in the interwar period, not Fascism or Nazism: 'Britain's secret intelligence service MI6 [...] continued to see the Soviet Union as the main enemy through the middle of 1930s.'[44] The reason for this is that, 'Britain emerged by default as the only global power and thus represented the greatest long-term threat to the survival of the Soviet regime.'[45] Stalin rightly sensed the difficulty with which Britain was trying to maintain the empire – he saw the latter as Britain's Achilles heel. Conversely, 'the Bolshevik threat to their empire had traumatised those who owned and ruled Britain. [...] One immediate and symptomatic side effect was a noticeable indulgence towards Fascism, because of its decisive suppression of Communists.'[46]

The new states of Eastern Europe and their societies were not particularly unusual in their reactions to these developments: some were more sympathetic to the new ideologies, some less. Each of these countries was hoping to obtain security guarantees ahead of the expected forthcoming military conflict, which soon came to be seen as inevitable.

---

43. Haslam, p. 4.
44. Ibid., p. 13.
45. Ibid., p. 61.
46. Ibid., p. 84.

Some, such as Hungary, began to slide towards their own form of nationalism, hoping perhaps to recover the pride and the territories lost in World War I. Czechoslovakia, Poland and Yugoslavia pursued a policy of thoroughgoing friendship with the Western Allies and also with the Soviet Union. They were very aware that they would be the first targets of Nazi and Fascist expansionist politics, as indeed they were.

In Yugoslavia, with the annexation of Austria in March 1938, Slovenians became the next-door neighbours of the Third Reich. This reinforced the appeasement efforts of Yugoslav government, including gestures to court the Nazi regime, some of them discriminating against Jews, at least on paper. Still, as late as December 1940, a conservative manifesto of the Slovenian People's Party read: 'We condemn capitalist and communist economic order. We reject a totalitarian state, formed in communism and fascism, which take away from other units of society and from individuals any autonomy and freedom.'[47] And already in 1933, the Slovenian conservative daily *Slovenec* wrote about 'big collectivist movements': 'Where are all these breeding grounds of revolutionary instincts and appetites supposed to end up, that Bolshevism, Fascism and Hitlerism, all children of the same mother, instil with such determination into the young generation? Where will materialise these new concepts about an absolute state, which on its own will, without regard for God's or natural law, forms its own legal norms?'[48] So awareness of both dangers seemed to be present in Central Europe. Given the fears of Slavic nations that stood in the way of the Nazi ideology this was understandable.

---

47. Cited in Žebot, C, *Neminljiva Slovenija*, Celovec, 1988, p. 74, (in Slovenian language).
48. Quoted in Rahten, A, Korošec, A, *Slovenski državnik kraljevine Jugoslavije*, Mladinska knjiga 2022, p. 354 (in Slovenian).

After the Leninist revolution, the Soviet Union itself was not ready for the war and was desperate to do whatever was needed to appease Hitler. 'Stalin realised that the working class of Europe were far too attached to bourgeois democracy to accept communism through violence',[49] and through Comintern, demanded that Communist parties abroad should not attack Fascism and Nazism, not even in Italy and Germany.

The West too, as explained above, adopted a policy of appeasement towards Hitler and, in the Munich accord of 1938, sacrificed Czechoslovakia, the richest and most developed democracy of what was then Eastern Europe. 'A quarrel in a far-away country between people of whom we know nothing', are supposedly the words used by the British Prime Minister Chamberlain to dismiss the problems in Czechoslovakia and to justify his deal with Hitler.[50] Haslam points out that this was not only about buying time, but also about Chamberlain's long-held view that too much money was spent on defence in the UK.[51] It would be up to Churchill to change that.

Among the countries desperate to avoid war was Czechoslovakia, which was, in many ways, a model country. It had a functioning democracy, a good economic base and an educated population, although the Czechs tended to look down on the much more rural Slovaks. It had a pro-Western foreign policy but its leaders, Masaryk and Beneš, were also not hostile at all towards the Soviet Union.

Poland was less a model democracy. Although there was a parliament and there were political parties, the country was effectively run as an authoritarian state under the leadership of

49. Haslam, p. 185.
50. As quoted in Adrian Hyde-Price, *The International Politics of East Central Europe* (Manchester University Press, 1996), p. 22.
51. Haslam, p. 296.

Marshal Piłsudski. The country was predominantly rural, with a weak middle-class, and it had many more economic problems than Czechoslovakia, not least because it had reconstituted itself out of three very diverse parts which, for almost 150 years, had belonged to three different states (Russia, Prussia/ Germany and the Austrian Empire). In addition, its Ukrainian minority was not treated properly and the country had territorial disputes, a major one with Lithuania (over Vilnius) and a smaller one with Czechoslovakia (over a coal-rich area). Foreign policy, though, was focused on averting the menace from both the Soviets and the Germans, so Poland signed treaties with both. Despite this, Stalin and Hitler attacked and partitioned Poland in 1939, making it very difficult for Poles to decide which of the two neighbouring states that invaded them was worst. And it was not only about occupation. In occupied Poland, the Soviet Union also launched a campaign of sovietisation, expropriating and nationalising big businesses.[52]

On the international stage, the alliance between the Soviet Union and Germany, as well as the consecutive partition of Poland, also needed some spin by the Comintern. Thus the word Fascism abruptly disappeared from Soviet vocabulary[53] and the official narrative became that of 'an imperialist war with respect to which the bourgeois of all the belligerent states are equally culpable.'[54] In words reminiscent of Putin's accusations against Ukraine in 2022, the Soviets talked about 'Fascist Poland, which has refused help from the Soviet Union'. As for France and Britain, they were said to have 'repulsed the Soviet Union in order to conduct a predatory war.'[55] In

---

52. Haslam, p. 335.
53. Ibid., p. 326.
54. Ibid., p. 332.
55. Haslam, p. 332.

fact, as late as January 1941 French Communists were told by the Comintern that 'conditions for liberating French people from under the yoke of the occupiers have, however, not yet matured.' They were asked instead to focus on domestic collaborators.[56]

Equally dramatic were the developments in the Baltic states and Finland. The Baltic states gained independence while caught between Germany and the Soviet Union. Latvia and Estonia were internationally recognised in 1921. Lithuanian independence was only won after a bitter row with Poland, which held on to Vilnius, the capital of Lithuania. Independence was short-lived, however: in 1940, the country was occupied by the Soviets as part of an agreement with Nazi Germany. It was then overrun by the Nazis and once again occupied by the Soviet Union. It only regained its independence in 1990. The fate of all three Baltic states was similar. In 1939 Soviet foreign minister Molotov bluntly said to his Estonian colleague: 'The Soviet Union is now a great power whose interest needs to be taken into consideration. I tell you – the Soviet Union needs enlargement of her security guarantee system; for this purpose she needs an exit from the Baltic Sea.'[57]

The same excuse was used against Finland (which could easily be described as an Eastern European country, given its geographic position and its relationship with Russia) and that country was eventually forced to surrender some of its eastern territories. Bordering neutral Sweden on the west, Finland's main worries about security also concerned the Soviet Union, not Germany. Following its experience in 1940, Finland sided with Germany (although it was far from embracing Nazi

---

56. Ibid., p. 369.
57. Haslam, p. 337.

ideology) and declared war on the Soviet Union in 1941, as did Hungary and Slovakia and (later) Romania. Who would have imagined that 80 years later Finland, neutral for many years, would again feel threatened by Russia and decide to join NATO?

In the whole Baltic area, countries were obliged to reach some kind of compromise with Nazi Germany in order to save themselves from what to them was the prime danger – the Soviet Union. In some cases – although this was not true everywhere – such compromise involved taking part in oppression and handing over local Jews to the Nazis, a reflection of the desperate position of these small countries caught between Nazi Germany on the one hand and the Soviet Union on the other. In Lithuania, approximately 94% of the nation's Jews perished in the Holocaust. In Latvia, almost the entire Jewish population died during the Nazi occupation.[58] (The French Vichy police too, in much less dramatic circumstances, assisted in the deportation of Jews and there were cases of collaboration with the Nazis in other Western European and Scandinavian countries. Many European nation-states do not exactly have a record in such matters that can bear too much examination.[59]) As far as the Baltics are concerned, the dominant narrative about this period of time is one of the

58. Naylor, A, *The Shadow in the East: Vladimir Putin and the New Baltic Front*, I.B.Tauris, 2020, p. 20.
59. 'Since 1945 the term "collaborators" has acquired a distinctive and pejorative moral connotation. But wartime divisions and affiliations often carried local implications altogether more complicated and ambiguous than the simple post-war attributions – of "collaboration" and "resistance" would imply... In France and Belgium, and also in Norway, resistance against the Germans was real... But not until the very end of occupation did the number of active resisters exceed the numbers of those who collaborated with the Nazis out of belief, venality or self-interest.' Tony Judt, *Postwar: A History of Europe since 1945*, William Heinemann: London, 2005, p.33.

'residents being cornered into self-defence after victimisation at the hands of two militarily superior invading forces'.[60] But this 'neat narrative can stir unease through these attempts to whitewash the past'.[61] Indeed, the prevailing memory in the region today is that of the brutality of the Soviet occupation, which Putin's Russia continues to skilfully use in its approach to the three countries,[62] accusing them of relativising the Nazi aggression and its crimes.

With all its internal problems, Yugoslavia, the other creation of the Paris Peace Conference, was also not a model democracy at the time but it was no worse than any of its neighbours. Italy turned Fascist and was openly hostile towards Yugoslavia, hoping to get control of the eastern Adriatic coast. Hungarian nationalism was radicalised and the country drifted towards the Axis powers. In Austria too, sympathies were with Germany. A dictatorship was imposed in 1933, the Prime Minister was assassinated the following year and the country was annexed by Nazi Germany in 1938, which was welcomed by the population. In the circumstances it faced, the Yugoslav leadership tried to please Hitler without compromising itself too much. It acceded to the wishes of the Axis powers under the condition that the country would not be drawn into the war, which was probably the best Yugoslavia could do. Nobody either could or wanted to offer it a meaningful security guarantee, and the Yugoslav Army was far too weak to stand alone against almost any of its neighbours. 'The Russians were understanding, less so the British [...] Stalin was bending over backwards to avoid provoking Germany.'[63]

---

60. Naylor, p. 16.
61. Ibid., p. 21.
62. Ibid., p. 152.
63. Haslam, p. 366.

However, the 1941 military coup d'état in Belgrade, which had what appeared to be wide popular support (and British intelligence backing), changed everything and enraged Hitler, who attacked Yugoslavia in April of that year.

Hungarian domestic politics during the inter-war years essentially consisted of a conflict between moderate conservatives and extreme nationalists. The loss (largely to Romania) of about a third of the Hungarian ethnic population and two-thirds of the country's former territory after World War I deeply influenced its foreign policy. Germany seemed the only country to have some understanding of Hungarian grief over these losses so, when the conservatives lost control of the extremists, Hungary turned openly pro-Fascist and joined the war on the side of Germany, regaining parts of Slovakia and Yugoslavia.

Romania greatly benefitted from Hungary being on the 'wrong' side in World War I and received the large province of Transylvania in the peace settlement. In 1923, it adopted a new constitution, boasted to be one of the most democratic in Europe at the time. Economic development was heavily dependent on domestic oil production: at the time Romania was one of the largest oil producers in the world.[64] But like Hungary, on the eve of World War II, Romania turned to the right in the hope that it might regain territories lost after World War I through its participation in war against the Soviet Union. It only changed its position in 1944.

Bulgaria leaned to the Axis powers as well, although it is also known that the Bulgarian Tsar, Boris III, resisted pressure to deport Bulgarian Jews. In Greece, a conservative dictatorship was established in 1936 but, in 1940, the government rejected

---

64. https://www.rferl.org/a/romania-oil/31510946.html

Mussolini's call for surrender. The country was then attacked and occupied by Germans and Italians.

In summary, in the absence of meaningful security guarantees by France, England or the Soviet Union, Eastern European nations found it impossible to resist German advances. Their fears would soon be justified: Nazi ideology treated Slavs much worse than Western Europeans. For that reason, casualties of war in Eastern Europe (including Greece) during the resulting Nazi occupation were far greater than anywhere else in Europe. (This includes the colossal human sacrifice made by the Russians.) For example, in Slovenia, 5.4% of the population was killed during World War II and in Poland 16%;[65] in Britain that percentage was 0.6%[66] and in France 1.35%.[67]

Europe of the post-war period, and its collective memory and identity, is based on the experience of Nazism, Fascism and the Holocaust. Generations of Europeans (perhaps excluding those in the neutral countries of Ireland, Spain, Portugal, Sweden and Switzerland) have been brought up knowing about the importance of the lessons for the future that their parents and grandparents learned from the experience of Fascism. For all but extreme right-wing groups, this remains unquestioned.

That is not the case with Communism. During the post-war period, left-leaning public opinion in Italy, Germany and (above all) France showed a persistent and sometimes almost

---

65. http://en.wikipedia.org/wiki/List_of_World_War_II_casualties_by_country#Casualties_by_country

66. John Corsellis, Marcus Ferrar, *Slovenia 1945 – Memories of Death and Survival after World War II* (IB Tauris 2005). This book is also suggested reading for those interested in the issue of reprisals against anti-Communists in Eastern Europe after World War II.

67. http://en.wikipedia.org/wiki/List_of_World_War_II_casualties_by_country#Casualties_by_country

religious trust in Communism of the Soviet type. And since Communism could at least be shown to have its origins in benevolent humanist ideas, which Nazism and Fascism could not, obvious parallels between the three ideologies, at least when it comes to the numbers of their victims, have often been rejected. Consequently, attempts to recognise the experience of totalitarian Communism as a part of the shared memory of Europe were not met with the enthusiasm that they deserved,[68] much to the regret of many in Eastern Europe (and to the satisfaction of the post-Communists in the region, which saw this as at least partial absolution of the past Communist regime). Still, in 2009, the European Parliament proclaimed the European Day of Remembrance for the victims of all totalitarian and authoritarian regimes, to be held every year on 23 August, the day of the infamous Ribbentrop-Molotov Pact. 'For many, this fateful day marked the beginning of a cycle of Nazi and Soviet occupation and violence,' conceded the European commissionaires in 2021[69] and a year later drew parallels with Putin's war in Ukraine[70] – for a good reason.

But the question of whether the three totalitarian systems were 'equal' persists. In fact, the three cannot easily be compared as they did not emerge simultaneously in the same countries, and

---

68. Norman Davies says: 'On the ideological front, Westerners are accustomed to thinking of the Second World War as a two-sided conflict, of good fighting evil. The Soviets had a similar dialectical view. They were the authors of the concept of anti-Fascism, which caught on in the West, encouraging the illusion that all opponents of Fascism were inspired by similar values. In reality, Soviet communism was every bit as hostile to Western democracy as it was Fascism...' From *Europe East and West,* Jonathan Cape, 2006, p.246.
69. https://ec.europa.eu/commission/presscorner/detail/en/STATEMENT_21_4283
70. file:///C:/Users/a490/Downloads/Statement_by_President_von_der_Leyen_on_the_Europe-Wide_Day_of_Remembrance_for_the_victims_of_all_totalitarian_and_authoritarian_regimes.pdf

they were also of very different duration. Comparison may be more valid between, say, Franco's regime in Spain and Tito's regime in Yugoslavia. Another difficulty in comparing the different systems arises from the fact that, although there were periods of violent anti-Jewish campaigns in the Soviet Union and also massive forced movements of entire ethnic groups which amounted to little less than genocide, Communism was not, by and large, racist in its ideology, at least not vocally. The enemy deserving extinction was the class enemy – to some this seemed a lesser evil. However, seen from the perspective of an individual (Eastern European) nation, Communism was a central experience that, in some places and with some people, even occasionally overshadowed earlier memories of Nazism and Fascism, the ones which remain the primary historical memories in the West. Cumulative numbers suggest that Communism, in its various incarnations, has been responsible for greater numbers of killings of its opponents worldwide than the other two totalitarian systems, especially when we include its victims in Asia.

This left-leaning electorate in Europe often thought that, at worst, there was a correspondence between American influence in Western Europe and Soviet influence in Eastern Europe. (This is a belief that is still alive and well in some quarters of post-Communist societies.) The other reason for the sympathy or at least the more lenient approach towards Communism was that (Soviet) Russia, as the driving force behind Communism in Eastern Europe, had also been an indispensable ally against Nazism that paid an enormous death toll for the victory – something that Putin has been skilfully using to justify marking out zones of interest in Central and Eastern Europe, and also as an excuse to deliberately play down Stalin's terror or his early collaboration with Hitler. It has also been a part of the Russian narrative of the war against Ukraine.

Of course, Stalin, always well aware of this leftist sympathy in the West, seized the opportunities offered to him, not least because Nazi Germany became a very serious, real and direct threat to Russia. With the advent of Communism, Russia's consistent strategic interest in Eastern Europe, which went back to the time of Peter the Great, was revived with the missionary zeal of the Communist revolution. To be fair to the Soviets, it should be said that Stalin was also afraid that right-wing or otherwise hostile governments in some Eastern European countries could facilitate German attack on Russia, which eventually, as we saw, was what happened. Hungary, Romania and Bulgaria hoped that siding with Germany might give them back territories lost in the aftermath of World War I. But Poland, the Baltic States and Finland were, above all, frightened by the prospects of Russian invasion. These countries did not want to be protected from the Germans by a Soviet occupation.

Unfortunately, the Soviet Union did not hesitate to address its own security concerns, even to the extent of signing a treaty with Nazi Germany at the expense of the smaller countries sandwiched between the two great powers. In addition, one must not forget the eagerness that still existed for the export of revolution: when the war between Germany and the Soviet Union eventually broke out, Moscow hoped that the fight against Nazism, and also the common Slavic roots, would make it much easier to install Communist or at least leftist governments in Eastern Europe. This is exactly what happened in 1945. Cynically, one might say that Eastern Europe got rid of the Nazis in four to six years, but it fell under Soviet control for 50 years. Eastern European fears of what the

107

Soviet Union might do actually became true; the pre-war fears of Communism turned into reality too – in the Eastern part of the continent. But how did it actually happen?

As we saw before, with Hitler on the rise, the Soviet Union was initially doing all it could to avoid conflict with Germany and asked Communist parties across Europe to sit by idly. It was not until the German attack on the Soviet Union in April 1941 that Communist parties around Europe were ordered to begin armed resistance. A part of Communist tactics to build up resistance movements was the idea of the so-called National Fronts – loose coalitions of all political parties that were willing to engage in resistance against the Nazis. The concept had its origin in France in the mid-1930s as a tactic in pursuit of communist control over a broad range of centrist political forces, as the Comintern realised that Communists in Western Europe could not carry out a revolution by themselves. In the new circumstances of Nazi attack, these coalitions were meant to gain broad public support for armed resistance movements as well as for the Communist parties to assume the pivotal and exclusive role in these Fronts – at gunpoint, if necessary.

This Soviet strategy was not always successful and local left and centrist political forces occasionally acted against the expectations of Moscow. In Poland, there was a strong resistance movement that was not associated with the Communists. It was much the same in Czechoslovakia, where the resistance focused on intelligence gathering, sabotage and Czechoslovak soldiers joining Allies abroad. In Slovenia, Communists assumed the leading role in the resistance and did so by physically eliminating not only those who decided to wait, but also many of those who were ready to fight against the Nazis and the Fascists but did not want to be associated with a Communist revolution. This created impossible, absurd situations in which the anti-Communist side even asked the occupying forces for arms in order to protect themselves from Communist terror; in turn then the Communists accused the anti-Communists of treason. Even today, this is still a source of controversy and divisions among historians and ordinary people in Slovenia and elsewhere.

Once the British and Americans realised that the most imminent threat to the liberal order was coming from Nazism and that, consequently, the Soviet Union would have to be brought into the war to beat Hitler, they became ready to deal with the Soviet Union, including to trade Soviet influence over Eastern Europe for Soviet military involvement. As early as 1943, in Tehran, Churchill and Roosevelt consented to Stalin's territorial request for the Baltic States, eastern Poland and Bessarabia (the eastern part of Moldavia). It appears that even Roosevelt downplayed the sinister nature of Moscow's demand for a zone of influence over Eastern Europe, and considered such a demand legitimate. Part of the Soviet argument, as described above, was that some of the Eastern European countries were hostile to the Soviet Union and were desperate enough to be ready to allow the transportation of German troops across their territories. But the Soviets acted just the same in Czechoslovakia which was friendly to Russia.

The decision to include the Soviet Union in the alliance against Nazism and Fascism also meant that Western Allies gradually came to acknowledge as legitimate various Communist-led resistance movements in Central and Eastern Europe, who yearned for recognition, hoping that this would in time lead to their legitimacy as a future government after liberation. The Western allies had no interest in discerning complex local situations nor time to spend on them. There is even some evidence to suggest that, in these contacts with local

Communist resistance movements, the British at least made use of their own left-leaning army officers, who relayed back home a rosy picture of these movements, one that Western governments could tolerate.[71]

In acting as he did, Roosevelt was ignoring the advice of military observers in Moscow, mistakenly thinking that Russia would democratise itself soon.[72] But it was Churchill who, on a visit to Moscow in October 1944, proposed spheres of influence in Eastern Europe to Stalin on a piece of paper. This is how Churchill describes the meeting in his own memoirs:

At ten o'clock that night we held our first important meeting in the Kremlin... The moment was apt for business, so I said, 'Let us settle about our affairs in the Balkans. Your armies are in Rumania and Bulgaria. We have interests, missions, and agents there. Don't let us get at cross-purposes in small ways. So far as Britain and Russia are concerned, how would it do for you to have ninety per cent predominance in Rumania, for us to have ninety per cent of the say in Greece, and go fifty-fifty about Yugoslavia?' While this was being translated I wrote out on a half-sheet of paper:

Rumania
   Russia 90%
   The others 10%
Greece
Great Britain (in accord with USA) 90%
   Russia (10%)
Yugoslavia 50–50%

---

71. See, for example, Arnez, J, *Slovenia in European Affairs: Reflections on Slovenian Political History*, League of CSA, New York, Washington, 1958, pp. 103 – 116.

72. McCauley, p.11.

Hungary 50–50%
Bulgaria
  Russia 75%
    The others 25%
I pushed this across to Stalin, who had by then heard the
translation. There was a slight pause. Then he took his blue
pencil and made a large tick upon it, and passed it back to us.
It was all settled in no more time than it takes to set down.[73]

It may be that Churchill could not have imagined that what he himself later called the Iron Curtain was going to be so devastating for the nations to the East of it, although he must surely have had detailed reports from Moscow about how Communism worked in practice. But one cannot escape the impression that, just as Chamberlain had been prepared to turn his back on Czechoslovakia, Churchill considered Eastern Europe a worthwhile bargain for the greater good – victory over Nazism, for which so many British lives were sacrificed too. One could also come to a further conclusion: that such an exchange would probably have not been possible had the image of a *lesser* Europe not already existed in the Western European mind.

The now infamous Yalta meeting in February 1945 confirmed the Soviet influence over Eastern Europe. Still, the clauses in the Yalta Treaty, which concerned the composition of provisional governments in Eastern Europe, were, at least in the case of Poland, differently interpreted by Churchill and Roosevelt on the one hand and Stalin on the other. While in Czechoslovakia there was genuine, large-

---

73. Winston Churchill, *Triumph and Tragedy* (Houghton Mifflin, Boston, MA, 1954) as cited in McCauley, p. 116.

scale public support for the local Communist party (though not for its future dictatorship), in Poland and other countries in Eastern Europe the Communists were only able to come to power because of Soviet support and manipulation or, as in the case of Yugoslavia, because of the dominance that the Communists forcibly imposed on the resistance movement. Their recognition as a legitimate force and interlocutor by the Western allies played an important role in this.

Thus while the British and Americans (with some help from various national resistance movements) liberated Western Europe and helped restore democracy there (even in Germany), large parts (though not all) of Eastern Europe, with the exception of Yugoslavia, were finally liberated by the Soviets, though with the considerable support of local resistance, Communist and non-Communist. Once their military presence was established, the Soviets certainly had no desire to help restore the institutions of liberal democracy that *had* existed, however imperfectly, in most Eastern European countries before World War II. Instead, Soviet puppet governments were established that were even obliged to refuse the generous offer of the American Marshall Plan for the aid and reconstruction of Europe.

Ravaged by Nazism and Fascism, Eastern Europe, finally liberated, did not enjoy its freedom long. In fact, within a few months or, at most, a couple of years of liberation from Nazism and Fascism, the region was forced into a new totalitarian system. In most countries, the shell of the national state remained (except in the Baltic countries which were annexed by the Soviet Union) but it was empty of freedom again. Soviet-style Communism spread all over Eastern Europe, the Iron Curtain was drawn, contacts with the West were cut and the region sank into oblivion. Members of various anti-

Communist movements went into exile. Many were not lucky enough to escape and became victims of mass purges. Both the exile and the purges significantly altered the political and social landscape for generations – the situation amounted to a policide. Central and Eastern Europe was abandoned and left at the mercy of the new rulers and their Soviet mentors. And in the eyes of Western Europeans, the region was labelled once again an alien, inhospitable, almost non-European place. It would remain so until the late 1980s.[74]

---

74. Norman Davies wrote: '...historians have a problem. Somehow they must find a way of describing a complicated war in which, after several twists and turns, the combined forces of Western democracy and Stalinist tyranny triumphed over Nazi Germany... At the same time, without minimising the Western contribution, they must emphasise that Stalin's triumph had nothing to do with freedom and justice, and that by Western standards the overall outcome was only partly satisfactory. It is a tall order. To date, no one has succeeded.' Quoted from *Europe East and West,* p. 248.

The Communist Effect:
The Creation of Eastern Europe

Not only in Eastern Europe, but in another part of the European periphery, in Portugal and Spain and then soon in Greece too, authoritarian systems continued after World War II. In fact, there are some interesting parallels between Eastern Europe and other fringes of Europe. As the authors of a book with a suggestive title 'Peripheral Identities' conclude, 'Portugal, Spain and the Eastern European countries experienced long-lasting totalitarian regimes and only turned to Europe after the collapse of their respective dictatorships.'[75] In the case of Spain, the memoires of Leopoldo Calvo-Sotelo, one of the leading figures of Spain's accession to the European Union, attest that the process of *transición* and rapprochement to Europe was equally marked by internal discussion of both Europeanising of Spain and Spain's contribution to European identity.[76]

Moreover, even 'the creation of identity in all of these countries is strongly influenced by their long experience of dictatorships during the last century and also by the European

75. Pinheiro, T, Cieszynska, B, Eduardo Franco, J, (ed.), *Peripheral identities, Iberia and Eastern Europe Between the Dictatorial Past and the European Present*, Pearlbooks, 2011, p. 15.
76. Leopoldo Calvo-Sotelo, *Un europeísta en la Transición*, Instituto de Estudios Europeos, Madrid, 2019.

integration'. The authors, however, observe an important difference in 'the fact that the revolution in Portugal and the democratic transition in Spain came about themselves, whereas in Poland, the Czech Republic and Romania the advent of democracy was also the advent of political sovereignty.' They conclude that the construction of national identity in Eastern Europe was more influenced by disassociation (from the Soviet Union or Yugoslavia) and at the same time by the idea of Europe, which is seen as a disassociation from the East. In their view too, Eastern Europe 'become a more ideologically based term' than the term Iberia, which is largely geographic.

Theirs could have very well been the fate for Eastern Europe after World War II, but history travelled down a different path. At the end of the war, generously helped by the presence of Soviet troops, Communist parties came into power in all the countries behind the Iron Curtain, thus consummating the agreement on spheres of interest between the great powers, and effectively creating what we have known ever since as Eastern Europe. Sometimes this happened through (more or less manipulated) elections, sometimes by threats and blackmailing of democratic politicians who gradually left or were removed from the political scene.

In Yugoslavia, Communism legitimised itself above all by the Communist-led partisan resistance movement, which forcibly monopolised the struggle. Tito violently eliminated or skilfully discredited other political competitors and was recognised by the Allies as the local coalition partner. Later on, because of the 'fifty-fifty' agreement, Tito was allowed to play Stalin in his own backyard: in Yugoslavia, the immediate aftermath of the war was marked by the mass summary executions of Tito's political opponents. Tens of thousands at least, and probably many more, Yugoslav anti-Communist troops are believed to have perished in massacres in the dense woods of south-east Slovenia, near (once German-populated) Kočevje and elsewhere, in the early summer of 1945. By some estimates possibly as many as 200,000 died in total (in Kočevje and other places), some of whom were handed over to Yugoslavia by the British Army stationed in Austria, either by force or under the pretext of being moved to Italy after they had fled to Austria. (British Quaker John Corsellis provided us with a sympathetic account of the tragic fate of these refugees in his book *Slovenia 1945: Memories of Death and Survival after World War II,* IB Tauris, 2010.) So many years later, Slovenian forensic scientists are kept busy discovering hundreds of illegal mass-graves and the national psyche has not yet come to terms with what happened – or does not want to: this was the most radical 'cancel culture', though not unheard of in other parts of post-war Europe at the time. Such pogroms were largely kept secret at the time but local Communists attempted to legitimise them by smearing anti-Communists as Fascists and collaborators with the Nazis. (Some of them actually were but they represented a very small minority.) At the same time, anti-Communists effectively committed political suicide when they allowed themselves to be forced into what they termed 'technical' collaboration with the occupiers (something that happened in Western Europe too). This was indeed an irony, as these people were often Anglophiles, who hoped that Slovenia was going to be liberated by the British and the Americans, not by Communist partisans or, even worse, by the Soviets. Their worst nightmare – which in the light of the Nazi campaign was dismissed by the Allies as of secondary importance at best and as betrayal at worst – actually came true. Their fears had not been exaggerated at all, quite the contrary; but they could have not imagined either the pogroms or the Orwellian style of government. Soviet-type Communism did come to Europe, but to its Eastern part, with Western consent given in Yalta. And not only that: Communist parties in the West grew in strength, in particular in France and Italy, which was causing some concern throughout the Cold War, especially to Americans. The Soviet Union's colossal loss of human lives during the war was rewarded with domination of Central and Eastern Europe and even with strong Communist parties in the West.

The Communist systems imposed after World War II in Central, South-Eastern and Eastern Europe had much in common but, across the region and over the decades in which they existed, they were not all exactly the same. The Hungarian uprising of 1956 and the Prague Spring of 1968 were able to take place because of the strong, liberally minded middle class which existed in these countries (at least in their capital cities) and which had a pre-war tradition of democratic life. In Poland, the Catholic Church, because of its strong traditions, featured as the most important informal opposition force. In the Baltic countries, their inclusion in the Soviet Union was, in fact, an annexation and it was followed by a mass immigration of Russian-speakers (and forced emigration of unreliable elements of the local population to the Russian Far East), with the purpose of changing the ethnic structure of the populace. The consequences of this still resonate today in the issue of the Russian community in the Baltic states. By conservative estimates, Soviet mass deportations saw between 200,000 and 400,000 people expelled by force from the Baltics and moved to Siberia and Kazakhstan.[77] On the other hand, the (forced?) migration of ethnic Russians to the Baltics results today in around 6% of the population in Lithuania being ethnic Russian

---

77. Naylor, p. 16.

and almost a third in Latvia and Estonia.[78] Luckily, 'their supposed loyalty to Russia is far from black-and-white.'[79]

In Yugoslavia, which was, apart from Albania, the only country of the former Communist bloc that was not in the Warsaw Treaty, the Communist regime was generally believed to be softer. Tito was even proposed for the Nobel Peace Prize. Yet his Yugoslavia had prisons full of political opponents and even a concentration camp on a barren Croatian island, next to the island of Rab, where the Italian Fascists ran a concentration camp only a couple of years before. In fact, this notorious Goli Otok camp was set up precisely when Tito decided to break with Stalin (or vice-versa), as he wanted to imprison those of his political opponents who were the most faithful to Stalin and therefore, in one sense, perhaps the most genuine Communists. Hundreds died there between 1948 and 1963 in the most dreadful circumstances, akin to prison camps in North Korea. Tito's dictatorship could probably be best compared with those of General Franco in Spain or General Pinochet in Chile but Tito, himself titled the Marshal, can certainly be held responsible for many more victims than these counterparts from the opposite side of the political spectrum.

It is important to understand that living under Communist rule in, say, Poland could be quite different from living under it in Hungary or Slovenia. These differences also help to explain variances in developments in different Eastern European countries after 1990. While, for example, from the perspective of religious freedom in Soviet-dominated Poland, one was free to attend religious services, in Slovenia

---

78. Naylor, p. 6.
79. Naylor, p. 153.

a teacher in a small town had to attend mass in a nearby city in order to avoid bullying at work. And Christmas was not a public holiday in Slovenia as it was in Czechoslovakia even though the country was almost overwhelmingly Catholic. On the other hand, while in Slovenia the Communist authorities left the Church a relatively high degree of autonomy in internal matters, in Czechoslovakia, the priestly occupation was regulated and vicars salaried by the State. As a result, a parallel underground Church was formed by those that wanted to remain independent – Tomáš Halík, the famous Catholic philosopher was one of its priests. The underground life in the then Czechoslovakia is also described in Roger Scruton's fictional *Notes from Underground*.

The experience above the ground also varied through the years of the Communist dictatorships. A joke about the Communist government could earn you years in prison in 1950s Slovenia but, in the 1980s, it would cost you a fine or, at most, a conditional sentence. The following is the experience of my own family.

My father's father was born at the end of the nineteenth century in a village that is today 20km from the Italian border, not far from the village of Vrhpolje, which I mentioned in the first chapter. He was born as a citizen of the Austro-Hungarian Empire. In World War I, he served in the Austrian army and, during a battle in the Tyrolean mountains, he lost his lower leg. As a result, he had to give up hopes of taking over the family farm and instead he went to Ljubljana to be trained as a watchmaker. There he met his future wife and returned to a small town near his native village. By then, he was a citizen of the Italian Kingdom, as Italy got a chunk of western Slovenia as a reward for turning its back on its former ally, Austria, during World War I. (This is how Vrhpolje, together with the famous battle at Frigidus, ended up in Italy.) A few years later, the Fascists came into power in Italy. In the ethnically mixed territory of the Trieste/Trst region, the Fascist ideology, often laughed at, translated into a very real terror directed against ethnic Slovenians, a long time before anywhere else in pre-World War II Europe suffered anything similar: the Slovenian language was banned from public use and the church became the only place where it was tolerated. Fascist militias ravaged villages in the wider Trieste/Trst region, molesting the local Slovenian population: during one such expedition, a Slovenian musician was forced to drink machine oil until he died. There were documented cases of Italian teachers spitting into the mouths of children that dared to speak Slovenian in school. Scores of Slovenian opponents of the Fascist regime were imprisoned, tortured or confined to remote parts of Italy. Four members of the secret Slovenian resistance movement were executed – those that a century later would be honoured by the Italian President. This was most probably the first antifascist movement in Europe and Slovenians in Italy the first victims of Fascism in Europe. In 1938, the movement even came close to assassinating Mussolini at Kobarid, site of the famous World War I battle known as Caporetto in Italian. According to a source, British intelligence convinced the man commissioned for the task not to proceed, allegedly to save the Munich accords.[80]

In those years, Fascism inspired the then little-known Slovenian writer Vladimir Bartol to produce *Alamut*, a fascinating story set in medieval Iran and depicting a militant religious sect. The work, which is above all a thinly veiled criticism of totalitarian systems and ideological violence,

---

80. Rutar, B, *Krik mačehe*, Mohorjeva založba Celovec, 2011 (in Slovenian).

Fascism in particular, was rediscovered in the aftermath of 9/11 due to what many saw as a prophetic account of Islamic fundamentalism and terrorism. In 2005, the book was included by the Spanish daily *El Pais* among the 50 greatest works of historical fiction and was published in English as well (Scala House Press, 2004).

Another artist of that time, Tone Kralj, a painter, gave himself the task of decorating small village churches across the Slovenian ethnic territory in what was then Fascist Italy. His frescos skilfully depict disguised versions of Mussolini and other Fascist frontmen, wearing the robes of Pontius Pilate and other figures complicit in Jesus' death.

In 1941, Fascist Italy made another move eastwards and occupied most of Slovenia. At home, my father's family supported the (Communist-led) resistance movement during World War II without knowing much about the Communist agenda behind it; for Slovenians in the Italian-occupied areas, national liberation and the fight against Fascism took precedence over any other consideration. Even so, after the war, the family was put under surveillance because of its Catholic connections. My father left teaching because of the pressure and went on to become a dentist.

My mother's family ran a relatively large farm in central Slovenia, near what was then the border between Yugoslavia and the Italian kingdom. During World War II, this family also largely supported the resistance movement led by the Communists but some of the extended family joined the anti-Communist forces too. Two of her uncles lost their lives in the post-war massacres. After the war, despite their support for the resistance, large areas of the family estate were confiscated.

Politics was often discussed in our home but we soon learnt to live double lives. In school, we had to join in the praises of the resistance movement, the Communist Party and Tito. Religion, let alone politics, could not be discussed at all – even the word Christmas could not be mentioned.

Of course, not everyone in Slovenia (or, for that matter, in other Eastern European countries) felt the same way about the Communist system as my family did. As well as those who were obviously corrupt, there were many people who, because of family tradition or for other reasons, sincerely believed in the system. Among the Party members there were some genuinely honest people. Some individuals among them, though few, even revolted and paid the price. And then there were the kinds of pragmatic individuals that are found in every society, who simply adapt to the situation, never raise their heads above the parapet, never speak up and just want to get by. It is important to realise this in order to understand that the return to democracy in the 1990s was not greeted with equal enthusiasm by all strata of society. I am not just speaking here of Party apparatchiks but also of a number of people who simply got used to the system and were not particularly interested in changes, especially if it meant uncertainty about their jobs or the availability of affordable housing. For the system was not totally bad. There was work for all, a free health service and affordable social housing. In 1960, the GDP of Yugoslavia was 2,437 dollars per capita. In Austria it was 6,519, in Italy 9,719, in Germany 10,839 dollars. It was 3,072 in Spain, 2,956 in Portugal, 3,146 in Greece and 4,282 dollars in Ireland. Yugoslav average GDP was, however, lower than that in Bulgaria (2,912), Hungary (3,649), Poland (3,215) and, of course, Czechoslovakia (5,108 dollars), and only higher than that in Romania.

Twenty years later, the average Yugoslav GDP was 6,063 dollars, Slovenian GDP around twice the figure. (For comparison: Irish GDP then was 8,541 dollars, while the Czechoslovakian average was only a little bit less – 7,982 dollars.) This means that, in the post-war period, Eastern Europe was seriously lagging behind the core of Western Europe, though the Czechs and Slovenians were at about the income levels of Spain, Portugal, Greece and Ireland.[81]

However, the difference between Eastern and Western Europe became significant after the 1980s. For 1990, the estimate for GDP for the Czech Republic alone stood at 8,895 dollars and for Slovenia 11,404. At the time it left Yugoslavia, Slovenia was richer than Greece (9,988) and Portugal (10,826) and it was almost at the level of Ireland (11,818 dollars), all measured in Maddison's 1990 international dollars. Eleven years later, in 2001, Slovenia's GDP (in the same units) was 13,843 dollars and the Irish GDP was 23,201 – such was the dramatic success of the Celtic Tiger in the EU and, on the other hand, the cost of transformation in Slovenia!

For Yugoslavs there was also free foreign travel: from about the 1970s, we had this unique possibility of travelling freely abroad, as much as we wanted, with the exception of openly vocal opponents who were denied a passport. When Yugoslavia opened its borders with what was then Western Europe, Slovenia, bordering Italy and Austria, profited the most. Slovenians were the lucky ones in the Communist world. Shopping in Italy or Austria was a fortnightly occurrence. We looked for the products that were not easy to find in the then Yugoslavia or were cheaper abroad, such as Sicilian oranges, bathroom tiles, electronics or fashionable clothes, jeans above all, usually at the lower side of the price scale and in the

---

81. The estimates are taken from Ljubo Sirc's book *Iščemo podjetnike* (GV, 1996), in the Slovenian language.

limited quantities allowed by the Yugoslav Customs. But it did not end with shopping. Books on politics that were banned in Yugoslavia, and printed by ethnic Slovenian publishing houses in Italy and Austria, or by political exiles in the USA or Argentina, were often hidden in the boxes of washing powder that were brought back across the borders on shopping expeditions. In other words, Slovenians were looking for all those artefacts of material, cultural and spiritual normality that their fathers and grandfathers knew in earlier times. The re-emergence of democracy and independence in the 1990s, and the accession to the European Union in 2004, therefore, represented a return to the normality of previous generations, not a venture into entirely uncharted territory. While other countries of the former Communist bloc were not as lucky in terms of travel abroad, the desire for such artefacts of normality was the same, even if they did not have the same opportunity to indulge in it. They still had the possibility of listening to short-wave BBC radio programmes (where Karl and Dora worked), to German Deutsche Welle or the Voice of America. I myself have warm childhood memories of the Slovenian ethnic minority radio programme from Trieste/Trst. By the way, these foreign stations also received considerable attention from the Yugoslav secret services, above all those young people posted to them as interns from Yugoslavia.

The other very important aspect of the open Yugoslav border was trade. Slovenia, the only Yugoslav republic bordering Western Europe, which had a relatively strong industrial tradition from the time of the Austro-Hungarian Empire, benefitted the most. It became the greatest Yugoslav exporter and the richest Yugoslav republic – and probably also the wealthiest nation in the whole Communist world. It was precisely because of the opening of the borders and the slightly less rigid Yugoslav economic system that we left Czechoslovakia economically behind during the post-war period. After 1990, Slovenia suddenly emerged as the richest of all the new independent states.

Returning to the subject of shopping abroad, Trieste/Trst, once frightened by the prospects of being taken over by Tito, thus became a consumer Mecca for Yugoslavs. This city, tucked in a short stretch of Italian territory under the Kras plateau, started to make a good living out of Yugoslav shoppers. For those on a budget, there was a particular part of the Trieste/Trst centre, around the old marina, where every imaginable type of Asian-made cheap good was on sale. The place, called Ponterosso, attracted scores of Yugoslavs, particularly from the southern parts of the country, who were easily recognised by the large plastic bags they carried to their cars and buses. Although they were fuelling the local economy (this was one of the reasons for the lack of enthusiasm for a democratic and independent Slovenia among some in Trieste/Trst, for whom it meant a loss of business), their shabby image, together with old ethnic prejudices from the Fascist era, made them targets of contempt for local right-wing groups and wider. These became even more convinced of their racial superiority over the 'Slavs', a term they indistinguishably used for Slovenians, Croats and all other Yugoslavs in the Trieste version of the 'Eastern Europeans' label.

On the other hand, 'Eastern Europe' was a good bargain for Yugoslavs in those times, and long weekends in Prague or Bratislava by coach were very popular. People brought back large quantities of fine Czech china and other goods. As a thriving economy before World War II, the Czech Republic was particularly badly hit by Communist economic policies when compared with other nations.

On the other hand, Czechoslovakia and Poland had strong opposition movements in the final decades of Communism. Intellectuals and students were meeting in private homes or in semi-private offices and cafés to hold lively discussions about every possible political issue, sometimes supported by Western intellectuals courageous enough to venture beyond the Iron Curtain – Roger Scruton was one of them. Writers and other intellectuals were spearheading democratisation in all Eastern European countries – this was almost a cultural revolution.

Interestingly enough, this did not occur on the same scale and intensity in relatively well-off Slovenia. There, a much more sophisticated socialist regime cleverly propelled to the fore a generation that had succeeded the warriors of the revolution, hoping that letting them indulge in arts and civil initiatives short of demands for democratic changes would prevent the return of a 'bourgeois' democracy and 'reactionary' mainstream art and civil society. This too had some specific consequences for Slovenian transition.

There is one more concept that needs to be included in a full picture of Communist Eastern Europe – that of the diaspora: the emigrants. As mentioned earlier, many anti-Communists of different colours – like Karl and Ljubo from the Prologue – fled Eastern Europe during the early years of Communism. Because these were usually highly-educated people and patriots, they soon established ethnic associations and even political parties and shadow parliaments in exile. The Slovenian political emigrants in Argentina, smeared as traitors by the Communist authorities, developed an impressive system of schools, crèches, companies, publishing houses, radio stations, etc. – all in the Slovenian language. Scores of third- and fourth-generation children speak fluent Slovenian.

(Poles all over the world have created even larger and more influential ethnic communities.) By the nature of things, these were, of course, people of staunch conservative views (as well as some liberals like Ljubo), and it was thus within the ranks of European Christian Democrats that they managed to find partners in the West who would listen to them. In fact, the all-European organisation of Christian Democratic parties even set up a committee to deal with the issues of Central and Eastern Europe where exiled politicians had the opportunity to meet Western politicians and lobby for their cause. (In the early years of the Cold War some of these exiles were also useful to the Western intelligence services.) In the late 1980s, many of them – by then growing old – served as links between Western politicians and government officials on the one hand and the new democratic political establishment that was emerging in Eastern Europe on the other.

These political emigrants did not, however, always find their homeland very welcoming. They were vigorously opposed by former Communists, who labelled them as traitors and extremists, but even the new democratic politicians sometimes found their presence embarrassing. They saw them as out of touch with the local situation, and harbouring expectations of what the new democracies could deliver that were simply too high, especially concerning the removal of all traces of Communist regime and redressing their losses, material and otherwise.

After the democratic changes and in particular after the entry of eight Central European countries into the EU, many of these countries would again see a similar emigration that, in the case of Bulgaria, Romania and the Baltic states, would amount almost to an exodus of the best and the brightest, now for economic reasons. In very much the same way as post-World

War II emigration depleted these nations of some of the most industrious and educated individuals, the post-enlargement emigration represented a similar brain drain that added to the sense of frustration, and fuelled social conservatism and populism among those left behind. The three Baltic states alone are believed to have lost 20% of their 1991 population.[82]

In Yugoslavia during the Communist times we also had another category of emigrants, the so-called guest-workers, who, in the 1970s, began to be attracted to Germany and, to a lesser extent, to Austria, Italy, Switzerland, France and Sweden. Just as some Irish went to the UK, it became customary for some Yugoslavs to travel to Germany for a couple of years to work (as a builder or nurse, for example) and then to return home. Many did so and invested the money they earned in a new house or a small independent business. Yugoslavs were joining a German scheme, called the *Gastarbaiter* programme, which sought to attract workers from Mediterranean countries for the fast-growing German economy, but this suited Tito's Yugoslavia too, as it provided a welcome source of foreign currency for his regime and prevented unemployment. The Yugoslav workers thus became a part of a larger Western European social experiment with migrant workforces that would decades later result in the issue of integration and also at least partly shape the continent's response to the 2015/2016 migrant crisis.

By the late 1960s, Slovenia developed to such an extent that it started to need a foreign workforce itself, above all in construction and services. From the 1970s onwards, buses of workers from Bosnia, Kosovo and other parts of the former Yugoslavia came pouring into Slovenia. (In 1962, the GDP

---

82. Naylor, p. 148.

per head in Slovenia was 195% of the Yugoslav average but was only 37% in Kosovo.[83]) They were the Slovenian version of guest-workers or an immigrant workforce, at times facing a degree of xenophobia, and at others positive discrimination against the locals in order to make a case for the official ideology of 'brotherhood and unity'. Lack of interest in learning Slovenian, taking for granted that their Serbian would be understood, was an issue, but many of them settled permanently and integrated. This was one of few immigrant experiences in Eastern Europe.

Slovenia appeared to be moving on despite Communism. Still, the net real incomes in relatively affluent Communist Slovenia only reached 1939 levels again in 1957. Because of the political and economic crisis after the death of Tito in 1980, incomes fell further after 1988 and thus, in 1991, were not much above pre-World War II levels.[84] One can imagine that the situation in the more isolated economies of Soviet-dominated Eastern Europe was even less rosy.

In the meantime, Budapest in 1956 and Prague in 1968 rose against the inhuman face of Communism. Both revolutions were quashed by Soviet tanks.[85] (As a response, Yugoslav ideologists developed the concept of 'Socialism with a human face'.) Some more positive signs came with the cautious normalisation of relations between West Germany and East Germany at the beginning of the 1970s. Then, in 1975, the

---

83. Ben Fowkes, *Eastern Europe 1945–1969, From Stalinism to Stagnation* (Longman Pearson, 2000), p. 92. A similar estimate was produced by Ljubo Sirc.

84. See note No. 22.

85. For the comparative economic study of fringe European countries it is interesting to note that some of the Hungarian refugees who, after the quashed uprising found shelter in Ireland, were taken aback by the living standards of late 1950s Ireland.

permanent Conference on Security and Cooperation in Europe (later transformed into what is now known as the Organisation for Security and Cooperation in Europe[86]) was established in Helsinki. Eastern European countries also joined it (they were allowed to do so by Moscow) and this marked the beginning of an easing of Cold War tension. In the meantime, Yugoslavia, which was not a member of the Warsaw Treaty, had been conducting a separate and largely independent foreign policy by launching the non-aligned movement in 1961, composed of mainly third-world countries with Yugoslavia and India as the leaders. Romania too was allowed a degree of independence in international affairs.[87]

But it was not only about security policy in Europe. Encouraged by the (rather timid) human-rights agenda of the Conference on Security and Cooperation in Europe papers, Czechoslovak political opponents, led by Vaclav Havel, founded the Charter 77 movement in that same year. Three years later, the economic difficulties in Poland reached their height and the Solidarity movement was founded. General Jaruzelski declared martial law after six months of protests, allegedly to prevent Soviet invasion. This was also the year of Tito's death, which was soon followed by troubles in Kosovo and then by the Yugoslav debt crisis.

Thus, while Yugoslavia was nearing a catastrophe, Central Europe was moving towards democracy. In 1989, Solidarity won the elections and formed a government, triggering democratisation movements all over Eastern Europe. Led by intellectuals, above all writers and former dissidents, people filled the streets and squares, demanding change. This process

---

86. www.osce.org
87. Gökay, p. 20.

took different forms in different countries across the region and different lengths of time to run its course, reflecting local conditions. But it is important to note that, in almost all places except Romania and Yeltsin's Russia, it was a completely peaceful process. Eastern Europe, as a political reality created by Communism and the Cold War, began to fall apart in a process that few, if any, could have predicted, let alone imagined its aftermath.

Part II: After the Fall

The Growing Pains of Transition

The democratisation process in Eastern Europe in the 1990s also represented an opportunity for the restoration of the national sovereignty of the Baltic states, the states of former Yugoslavia, and Slovakia. In fact, regaining independence was sometimes more attractive and emotionally stimulating than the much more demanding task of building a democracy, providing the much needed legitimacy for the painful transition.[88] For painful it was: there were obviously trade-offs between the stakes of market, welfare, democracy and identity, and these trade-offs would, from that moment on, significantly shape the developments of Central Europe.

In the Baltics, the necessary justification for the unpopular reforms was found 'around the flag of idealised visions of their interwar nations, states, and economic institutions. Conversely, the Soviet legacies were presented as dangerous obstacles to the most important task the reformers set themselves. [...] Baltic politicians, therefore, made the most radical break with the past, and paid little attention to the costs involved.' There was a different approach among the Višegrad countries where the reformers 'embraced the

88. Bohle, D, Greskovits, B, *Capitalist Diversity on Europe's Periphery*, Cornell University Press, Ithaca and London 2012, pp. 260 – 265.

socialist industrial legacies and qualified workforces as foundations for successful reindustrialisation...' This was important later on, when the economic crisis hit Europe, and over-reliance on Asian industry proved a burden. A distinct approach could be observed in Slovenia, where 'politicians were early on challenged by and had to learn to cooperate with a powerful labor movement, which had its own view on what elements of the inheritance ought to survive. Trade unions, center-left politicians, and the reformist bureaucracy backed by businesses that maintained strong links to the state have embraced the legacies of Yugoslav self-management and market socialism, and eventually transformed these into durable institutions of neocorporatist interest mediation.'[89] Such specific economic and political transition has much to do also with the peculiarity of the contemporary rule of law situation in Slovenia, as the next chapter will show. In short, 'the reliance on nationalism was most prominent in the Baltic states and Croatia. [...] even if nationalism has played a role in the Višegrad group and Slovenia, it has not been invoked as a single major legitimising force of the new order.'[90]

The transition process in Eastern Europe was taking place at a time when societies in the West had long ago moved beyond the concept of the nation-state as the main source of a state's legitimacy. In such a context, the new patriotism in Eastern Europe after 1990 was not always easy to comprehend. It often appeared out of touch with the spirit of the time in the rest of Europe. The drive to establish new nation-states by those small nations that had not had the chance to do so earlier in their histories (for example, in the nineteenth century that saw the

89. Ibid.
90. Ibid.

creation of Germany and Italy) was, in the early 1990s, often misunderstood in Western Europe as an expression of a will to fragment, a movement towards what has been portrayed as Balkanisation (one of those political terms wrongly associated with the Balkans[91]). The counter argument – that only sovereign nations can decide on joining transnational or intergovernmental organisations like the EU – did not sound strong enough, both because the world had, at the time, moved beyond traditional concepts of sovereignty and because most of these nations had only very limited experience, if any, of being a sovereign nation.

Furthermore, lurking timidly behind these developments and almost undetected at the time (conservative and Christian democratic parties in Europe were then at their full strength, and they were the ones that offered the most enthusiastic support to new political parties in the East) was also the region's social conservatism, to which I shall return in the following chapter, and to which national identity was of central importance. Part of the reason that, at the time, this social profile largely went unnoticed was also the equally and passionately pro-European character of the newly emerged political forces in Central Europe. For them, the return to Europe was a natural part of their staunch anti-Communism or anti-Soviet attitude.

Indeed, the new states from Central and Eastern Europe, once they joined the EU, became some of its most devoted members – at least that was the spirit in the 2000s and probably still in the early 2010s. There was a good reason

---

91. Maria Todorova in *Imagining the Balkans,* Oxford University Press 1997, notes that the term was not coined in the context of the Balkan nations' struggle for independence from the Ottoman Empire, but when the Austro-Hungarian and Russian Empires fell apart and this resembled the disintegration of the Ottoman Empire. (See pp. 32–35.)

for that: for the peoples and governments of Central and Eastern Europe the enlargement of 2004 was not (only) an enlargement of an already existing union. For them, it was a re-creation of a more wholesome Europe, one which could not exist without them, a return to the realities before Yalta and the Iron Curtain. It was also a confirmation of their essential European virtues and qualities. Before World War II, life in cities like Ljubljana, Prague, Budapest, Bratislava and Warsaw (as I have been trying to show throughout this book) was not substantially different from life in Vienna, Munich, Milan and Berlin. There were differences in the size and wealth of the cities, but the way of life and the mentality of the urban people were essentially the same. This is too often forgotten.

The case of the late Pope John Paul II, who was Polish, is a good example of the thinking in the region at the time: 'An injustice has been done to Poland and to the Poles by the misleading thesis of a "return" to Europe',[92] he wrote. Among the arguments in favour of the claim that the Poles (and, by analogy, other peoples in Central and Eastern Europe) have always been there as a part of Europe, he listed the early adoption of Christianity, the Polish contribution in wars against the Mongols and later the Ottomans (recall the chapter on the Balkans!), various Polish philosophers and, more recently, the Polish contribution during World War II. Poland was more courageous than the Western Allies, the pope argued: 'While the Western democracies deluded themselves into thinking they could achieve something by negotiating with Hitler, Poland chose to accept war, despite the clear inferiority of her military and technological forces. At that moment the

92. Pope John Paul II, *Memory and Identity*, Orion, 2005.

Polish authorities judged that this was the only way to defend the future of Europe and the European spirit.' One could add reference to the resistance movement of ethnic Slovenians in the early Fascist Italy.

It is remarkable how the Polish pope went beyond his religious mission and found it so important to advocate the partaking of Eastern Europe in the formation of Europe as a civilisation, including in the fight against Nazism, but also to point out the role of Christianity – something that at the time of writing did not yet sound out of place and politically incorrect, as it would today. (I will return to the theme of Christianity soon, as it is at the centre of conservative argument in Eastern Europe.)

In the eyes of Eastern Europeans, generations of Western Europeans have become too easily accustomed to thinking of themselves as Europeans in an exclusive way, even though neither Western Europe nor even the European Union can simply be equated with Europe. On the other side of the divide, Eastern Europeans never stopped thinking of themselves as Europeans and did not start thinking of themselves as Eastern Europeans until the Western Europeans told them that that was what they were. What the Polish pope wanted to remind his European audience was that the nations of Central Europe too are the heirs to Europe's Judaeo-Greco-Christian-Humanist culture. Obviously, the ways in which this culture was adopted were different in Eastern Europe as a whole and in the various nations within it. (There were also differences in the ways European culture expressed itself in Italy and in Britain, in Spain and in Sweden.) But that does not make Eastern Europe less European.

It is also true that in south-east Europe and 'Eastern Europe proper', the late arrival of Enlightenment ideas resulted in a slower societal development and less experience of liberal democracy, but even that does not make these countries less European, only less Western European.

For the pope then – and to many in Central Europe today – this cultural legacy, above all Christianity, was and still is the key link between the two parts of Europe. For that reason, the ongoing process of removing this shared legacy has been for some time also opening a gap between the East and the West, without almost anyone in the West paying attention or seeing it as a problem. Quite to the contrary: religious and Christian argument in particular has been again seen as an obstacle in what Canadian philosopher Charles Taylor famously christened as a 'secular age' in his seminal work with the same title.[93]

There is one other major issue complicating the already complex scene. The new challenge has been that Europe, and Western Europe in particular, began to be somewhat unsure about what actually constitutes European identity; gradually identity and values became all about various rights and liberties, notably in the intimate area, like sexual and gender identity, and reproductive rights. What was also new was that justification for these liberties, as well as for liberal democracy in general, is no longer to be looked for in Enlightenment ideas and classic liberalism, and even less so in the Roman, Greek and Judean roots of European civilisation, let alone Christian ones. Actually, the roots are not explicitly described anymore, but are believed to be found in radical individualism, as philosophically embraced by post-modern thinkers. This somewhat sudden and rather

93. Taylor, C, *A Secular Age*, Cambridge, Massachusetts: Belknap Press of Harvard University Press, 2007.

selective abandoning of references to the pillars of European civilisation has surprised and alienated Eastern Europe, who parted way with the Western half of Europe at a time (the end of World War II) when the classic liberalism of the Enlightenment began its slow decline to be replaced a couple of decades later by post-liberal, post-modern and certainly post-Christian society. True, in this new society, Eastern Europe had hardly taken any part in its creation. It could only attempt to copy it.

Moreover, with the approaching centenary of World War II and the last Holocaust survivors and Allied soldiers laid to rest, there have also been increasingly fewer references to the lessons of World War II. The war is now a distant memory.

But the legacy of the victory over Communism has been evaporating at an even faster pace and has now for some time been seen as something deserving no more than a passing acknowledgement. In any event, it has been increasingly seen as their (Eastern Europeans') victory.

As a result, the contribution of Eastern Europe to the formation of European identity has been minimised in many quarters, worthy of little more than polite acknowledgement. At worst, references to its historical contribution to Europe are taken as a historic curiosity and another confirmation of the region's social conservatism. At best, Eastern Europe's tragic experience of Communism and courageous victory over it are still honoured in speeches at solemn occasions, but with little real importance given to them. As the generation that brought about these changes is dying out, so is the memory of it – and the attachment of real significance to it. What is more, the Communist issue now seems to be used, at least in some places, as an excuse by the power-hungry populists of Eastern Europe trying to justify their capture of the state and attacks

141

on liberal democracy. Communism also became a taboo, very much like fascism.[94]

But has the Communist legacy indeed disappeared? Or is it still lurking in the very fabric of the post-Communist societies? Is it in any way still of relevance? Are its consequences still with us or are the conservative Eastern Europeans kicking a dead body?

The most serious blow that Communism delivered to Eastern Europe was not to the economy; it was to people's self-confidence.[95] Western European society is built on the premise of trust between people, on the assumption that people are, in principle, honest and trustworthy. Not so in Eastern Europe, where (at least in the past) an individual was treated with suspicion in most social situations. He or she could not be trusted as a matter of principle; their trustworthiness needed to be proved in advance. For all its talk about Humanism, Communism saw the diversity of individuals as the greatest danger to its grand project. The true message of Communism to an individual was unmistakable: the system treats you as a cog in the machinery of a society on its way to a perfect Communist world, so you treat other people like cogs too. And if I am not valued and appreciated as a distinct person but only considered as a replaceable cog, then why should I value my

94. Riemen, R, *To Fight Against This Age: On Fascism and Humanism*, W. W. Norton & Company, 2018, p. 32.
95. Koch and Smith in *Suicide of the West,* Continuum, 2006, also list among the six key features of the 'West' optimism and individualism, two traits that can loosely be identified with what I term self-confidence. At the root of optimism, Koch and Smith see myths of the autonomy of man, his essential goodness and the belief that creation is constantly progressing. Communism denies all these. An individual is only worthwhile as part of a collective. It is important to note, however, that both authors make it clear explicitly that the *West* in the title of their book also includes what is popularly referred to as Eastern Europe.

fellow citizens who share the same fate as cogs in a machine, and surely cannot be any better than me?[96] This emphasis on the mass society, 'the rise of the mass-man'[97] is something that connects Communism with Fascism. Everyday work routine (so often praised in the Anglo-Saxon/Protestant tradition as a virtue) was turned into a burden, a tiresome exercise which bore little relationship to one's social standing and could do little to affect it. Work, praised so highly in the Communist world, became of very little true value, an activity to be avoided, ineffective, and the products of it shabby and poor. On the other hand, what were glorified were the masses and the 'revolt of the masses',[98] the revolution. This is the reason why the Communist-led resistance to Nazis and Fascists during World War II has often been portrayed as a revolt, not as resistance. The emphasis was not on the resistance against the Nazis, but on the social revolution led in parallel, which in turn is retroactively legitimised through the resistance. It is therefore no coincidence that Svetlana Makarovič, a well-known writer and at the same time a leading figure of the contemporary leftist movement in Slovenia, continues to invoke the word 'revolt' in her activist engagement.[99]

---

96. This has been very well explained by Roger Scruton. Although he is making the case for national loyalty, the lack of what he terms 'accountability to strangers' was a feature of Communist societies and continues to some extent to be a feature of societies in transition. Scruton says that, in the transition process, 'almost as soon as democracy is introduced a local elite gains power, thereafter confining political privilege to its own gang, tribe or sect, and destroying all institutions that would force it to account to those that it has disenfranchised'. See Roger Scruton, *A Political Philosophy,* Continuum, London 2006.
97. Riemen, R, *To Fight Against This Age: On Fascism and Humanism*, W.W. Norton & Company, 2018, p. 41.
98. Ibid.
99. https://www.kinosiska.si/en/dogodek/svetlana-makarovic-with-guests/ (Retrived on 4 August 2022.)

This lack of self-confidence of the mass-man – of which a lack of personal responsibility is a corollary – has continued to impede the functioning of the state and society in many post-Communist countries, despite a changing culture and Generation Z's prevailing ignorance about the past. Personal responsibility was replaced by the actions of a man (or woman) as a part of the mass – the revolt.

This has had implications also in the economic sphere. The new political and economic system has unleashed the free spirit of enterprise, but this has certainly not been helped by the sad record of what has become known in Eastern Europe as 'wild privatisation', i.e. dubious, rigged privatisation, involving the use of insider information and a complete disregard for the position of the workers. In the often weak legal environment of the early transition period, this practice was usually possible because of the 'old-boys' network', i.e. the informal network of the business, political and even cultural elite from the Communist era which continued to hold power. To finance a (crooked) management buyout, a manager, probably a former party apparatchik, would have a far better chance of getting a loan with a bank than a 'stranger'. Such practices were also facilitated by the weak and dispersed ownership that could not exercise proper control of the management. For their part, the former political elite often made sure that legislation provided a sufficiently vague legal environment to shield their friends in the business elite from potential domestic and foreign competitors. Often the politically attractive argument of 'national interest' was used to support the creation of such legislation. All this, of course, came at the price of financing the now-reformed parties' political machinery that would return them to power every four years and thus help replicate the political elite. A survey of the various elites in the country, carried out in post-Communist Slovenia in 1995, has shown that the people who constituted the economic and cultural/artistic elite in that year were 89% the same as they were in 1988 before the changes. Only within the political elite was the equivalent figure lower – at 71%.[100] The case was much the same in Hungary and, to some extent, in Poland, although in the Czech Republic the former elite lost almost all of the little credibility and legitimacy it once possessed. Two decades later, there is a growing number of the conservative electorate in Eastern Europe that believes this replication of elites is alive and well.

In many societies in transition it took years before canny apparatchiks accepted normal ways of doing business and discovered that a good corporate culture is better – even for them – than murky business practices. (In the meantime, those playing by the rules suffered grave disadvantages.) Gradually, businessmen and politicians during the transition years came to look like responsible and respectable citizens, even in the eyes of foreign analysts and business partners, who might embody the virtues of stability, predictability and the right yields.

But, for those who were looked down on during the Communist years, seeing the same people in power again has been simply too much to bear. It has created frustration, augmented support for unconventional, often chauvinist, political parties and fuelled the kind of radical conservative emotions that put off foreign observers and analysts so much,

---

100. See Anton Kramberger, *Positional Elites in Politics, Economy and Culture in Slovenia During 1988–95: Summary Statistics on Elite Segments,* CESTRA, 1998. For other countries see Frane Adam, Matevž Tomšič, *Transition Elites: Catalysts of Social Innovation or Rent-Seekers,* Faculty of Social Sciences, University of Ljubljana (unpublished).

and strengthen stereotypes about Eastern Europe as a socially backward, illiberal and intolerant place. Fears of the return of Fascism were even expressed in some places.

Instead of a comeback of the exiled, ousted or in some other way disenfranchised former business and social elite, a new middle-class has been emerging, often out of the post-Communist circles, but these new rich have been only slowly acquiring the attributes of such a class, above all its sense of social responsibility. Little or nothing has been done in Eastern Europe in terms of positive discrimination for the previously discriminated to compensate them for the fact that the legacy of the former regime has allowed a small section of the population to achieve an (economic) advantage over everyone else. The political transformation has not taken things back to the beginning and created a level playing field for everyone. Such measures were believed to be impossible to implement.

At the heart of the economic debate in countries in transition was rather the question of whether their governments should undergo shock therapy or should manage the change to a market economy in a more gradual way. The American economist Jeffrey Sachs was among those who advocated a rapid approach, and he was a frequent visitor to Eastern Europe. On the other hand, the Nobel laureate Joseph Stiglitz was very critical of this argument and he has been able to put forward the examples of Poland, Hungary and Slovenia as countries which took the less painful road of a gradualist approach that led to greater social and political stability and faster economic growth in the long term.[101] The advocates of shock therapy admitted that their approach does indeed lead to a drop in

---

101. Joseph Stiglitz, *Globalisation and its Discontents,* Penguin, 2002, pp. 180–188. This partially overlaps with the analysis by Greskovits and Bohle.

individual living standards in the short run but that this type
of economic reform brings the promised gains later on. Using
a graph with consumption on the vertical axis and time on the
horizontal axis, they produced the so-called J curve, widely
spoken about in conservative circles in Eastern Europe. They
have also argued that a gradual approach in post-Communist
economies has benefitted exactly those kinds of people
described earlier: '[from] enterprise insiders who have become
new owners only to strip their firms' assets; [from] commercial
bankers who have opposed macroeconomic stabilisation to
preserve their enormously profitable arbitrage opportunities
in distorted financial markets; [from] local officials who have
prevented market entry into their regions to protect their share
of local monopoly rents; and [from] so-called local Mafiosi
who have undermined the creation of a stable legal foundation
for the market economy.' These were the unintended winners
in the transition process.[102] Still, Stiglitz concludes by labelling
these former Communist businessmen as 'pragmatists who
wanted to get ahead in the system. If the system required that
they join the Communist Party, that did not seem an overly
excessive price to pay.' He then continues: 'While some of
these "practical men" were ready to steal as much of the state's
wealth for themselves and their friends as they could get away
with, they were clearly no left-wing ideologues... It had taken a
long time for us finally to stop judging people by whether they
were or were not Communists during the old regime – or even
by what they did under the old regime.'[103]

With or without ideology, innovative privatisation has
created social tensions, has compromised both the market

102. Joel S Hellman, *Winners Take All – The Politics of Partial Reform in
Postcommunist Transitions,* World Politics 50 (January 1998), 203–34.
103. Stiglitz, pp. 167–168.

economy and democratic ideas, and ultimately created distortions in the markets, where small and medium entrepreneurs with no political friends were displaced by comrades in business. As we shall see in the following chapter, all these created fertile grounds (and sometimes just a good excuse) for the rise of populists in Poland and Hungary, and elsewhere, who continue to use the Communist argument.

But can former Communists really be blamed for all the troubles and vices of the post-Communist societies? Are they really the cause of the populism in Eastern Europe? Is there a danger of a return to Communism? To admit the truth, the new democratic political elites in Eastern Europe have not always lived up to their promises either. The first battalions of these usually consisted of uncompromising, often naïve idealists who had never run anything other than a literary society or a semi-illegal intellectual journal. (However, even the most experienced macroeconomists and policy analysts would probably not have been able to do much better in the circumstances.) What happened was that, all across Eastern Europe, a few years after the first democratic elections, pioneering democratic governments fell and were, by the late 1990s, replaced by political parties which had been fancily rebranded either by truly progressive ex-Communists or simply by those who were less scrupulous and did not mind laying spurious claim to being Western-style Social Democrats or even Liberals. This was certainly no ordinary comeback to Communism, but an advent of post-Communists, and the new political parties were at least partially to be blamed for that.

In some respects, the 1990s were not the best of times for new political forces in Eastern Europe to arise from the ashes. What happened in the meantime with the party political scene in Western Europe was a significant transformation, ending the post-war consensus of Christian Democrats and Social Democrats. This consensus has produced an unparalleled social state, a state that cared for an individual from cradle to grave. The left had become less radical, perfectly respectable and politically correct. The conservative camp moved closer to the centre and away from its Christian roots. But then, the oil crisis and the slowdown of the 1990s struck. People became less interested in low-tax policies and more in keeping their jobs and preserving a generous welfare state. The left understood all this well enough, while conservatives were busy thinking how – with birth-rates at a post-war low – to finance full employment and the same levels of social benefits. Flexicurity replaced the so-called social-market economy.

And there were, as already mentioned, changes in the cultural sphere too. Increasingly, the classic liberal mindset was given less space in academia and in popular culture. A post-modern world was being born, with critical race and gender theory, the 'woke', presented as scientific theory and occupying the academic space. While ethnic and class issues were largely gone, new group identities in apparent need of recognition started to emerge as subjects of academic research and study, especially in the sexual sphere.

In this context, along came a newly-liberated Eastern Europe with its own economic and social problems which it was very poorly equipped to solve. Its new, mostly conservative parties not only wanted to change the whole spectrum of economic and social policies, and the fabric of society; they also wanted to address all the injustices done during the Communist regime – from annulling politically-motivated court rulings to restoring forcibly nationalised property. They wanted to compensate all the many people who had been disenfranchised by the former Communist regime. But the stakes were too high. It was much easier for the former Communists to simply adopt the appealing image and message of the contemporary European left, knowing only too well that the majority of Eastern Europeans were not primarily interested in compensation for injustices; they were more concerned about keeping their jobs and preserving relatively generous public services that were free for all. And the left did not ask for additional sacrifices from the public in order to reach the living standards and private incomes enjoyed in the West. The left in Eastern Europe, at first discredited by the Communist legacy, was thus gradually becoming in tune with public sentiments at home, but also aligning with the prevailing spirits in wider Europe.

On the side of the new political forces, those seeking redress have in the early days of transition made use of 'lustration' – the removal from office of those who had been compromised by participation in the former regime. The former East Germany is known to have been most systematic in doing this. Others followed suit, with the intensity of the process being inversely proportional to the perceived softness of the former regime in a particular country. Generally speaking, throughout Eastern Europe, lustration was only halfheartedly implemented, and soon began to run contrary to the spirits of the time too.

In some countries, the process of lustration also swept editors and journalists from their positions. Despite such measures, the return of democracy has not also meant the return of truly free and unbiased media. The advantage of 'old boys' in business and media allowed for survival and, ultimately, continued dominance of the left-leaning media. There was only limited room for truly new and independent media – and also few trained journalists apart from those already in the job. As the political transition continued, efforts to make the media landscape more plural and transparent began increasingly to be seen as attempts by conservative governments to control the media, as if the declared and by now legislated freedom of expression was not enough. So the media became another area where the new democratic parties and conservative activists were increasingly out of tune with prevailing expectations in Eastern European societies, but also out of tune with the way of thinking in Western Europe, where the end of redress was expected. Transition was declared as ended with the entry of these countries into the European Union, so normalisation should follow. But now it appeared that they were the new democratic parties rocking the boat of constitutional order that was supposed to be untouchable.

As we shall see in the next chapter, distortions also continued in the area of government checks and balances. Skilfully, the former Communists have discreetly been spreading doubts about parliamentary democracy at a time when in the West liberal democratic governance has been challenged by populists and autocrats due to its perceived lack of effectiveness.

Moreover, as with the media, the dominant influence of old networks continued in the sphere of civil society. Of course, even the former Communist regimes used to have what looked like a civil society from the outside: a number of organisations from sport clubs, consumers' watchdogs and beekeepers' associations to United Nations' clubs, arts councils, charity organisations and peace institutes. But local party members were always given the task of ensuring that the 'right' people chaired these societies, and the state was only generous in financing them as long as they were giving value for money, i.e. providing the illusion of an independent civil society. During the political transition, some of these organisations proved to be extremely useful as shelters for discredited former

Communists. Another useful new role of these organisations has been to produce all sorts of 'independent' and 'expert' opinions and reports to be used as political ammunition by the ex-Communists against their political adversaries, providing a veneer of competent professionalism for decisions which have been made for purely political or private interest reasons. In addition, civil society organisations have been often established from above, assisted by the EU, rarely emerging from the grassroots. Thus backed by international institutions, often blindly, the left has re-emerged as the dominant force in civil society too.

On the other hand, little valuable 'infrastructure' of civil society was already in place for the new political elite to use. As a result, the presence of new conservative political forces was limited to politics, where – lacking political experience – they often appeared coarse, clumsy, off-the-mark, professionally incompetent and with no real support in civil society. Usually, the only organisation that the conservative politicians could occasionally count on was the Church, but even here the local situation varied greatly across Eastern Europe. In devout Poland, the Church was an important player and waved the flag for change. In the more secular Czech Republic, it was rather marginal. In Croatia, it was strongly on the side of the main new nationalist political party. Generally speaking, without the Church's support, there would not have been enough votes to elect the new political elites in Central Europe at the time of key changes. This was certainly true in countries with a strong Catholic tradition, where the Church was not only the biggest single victim of the former regime but also its firmest opponent, nurturing a deep ideological/philosophical opposition to the very principles of the Communist system. The liberal intellectuals who led the political changes in most of Eastern Europe were often out of touch with the conservative masses and they needed the Church and conservative intellectuals to motivate people and bring them to the polling stations. Still, over the years, association with the Churches became a liability, as they could no longer be of assistance in facing the increasingly post-liberal and post-modern society. The Churches themselves began to be overwhelmed by the unexpected and fast-advancing landslide of secularisation, and torn over the question of how to follow their missions in these new social circumstances, not least from a purely material point of view. The freedom suddenly seemed more of a challenge than an opportunity.

In any event, it would be rather superficial to portray the democratic changes in Central Europe in black and white terms, and to reduce it to a struggle between Communists and non-Communists. After all, individuals in Eastern Europe have reacted to the changes of transition in many different ways, reflecting their different places in society, as well as personal and family backgrounds. There are those who have never really trusted the new political parties and the changes that they have brought, and who remember the good old days with nostalgia, either because of the perks they used to enjoy or because their lives did not really change for the better (sometimes they became more difficult). This has given rise to support for various radical, extreme left and/or chauvinist parties, or for one of the reincarnations of the former Communist party. In the conservative camp, there are people who, whatever their present economic situations, continue to be staunch supporters of the new political parties, often with a strong anti-Communist rhetoric. Curiously, at the time of the changes in the early 1990s, these were usually also the strongest supporters of membership of the European Union, which they saw as a powerful weapon against the former Communist elites. Unfortunately, some of these enthusiasts have in the recent decade moved to occupy radical Eurosceptic or even xenophobic positions. And it is Euroscepticism and xenophobia where extreme left and extreme right movements often meet.

Then there are the nouveaux riches, sometimes with strong connections with ex-Communists who have reinvented themselves as liberals. The creation of this new social class was only possible where a strong urban tradition existed and circumstances allowed sufficient wealth to be gained.

Finally, there are those few who, after 50 years of leftist experimentation, still believe or hope for a genuine Social Democracy. Such a strong and genuine Social Democratic tradition exists in the Czech Republic, for example, despite their recent electoral setback.

The political landscape in the new democracies of Eastern Europe continues to change – something that we can also observe in the West. The transition from a Communist totalitarian system to a capitalist democracy was from many aspects a success, judged by macro-economic figures and the fact that the countries of Eastern Europe joined the EU and NATO. But this success also in many ways outpaced society's and many individuals' capacity to adapt to the changes. While some disproportionally benefitted from it, sometimes owing to undue comparative advantages rooted in the totalitarian past, others were left behind, often confused and frustrated. This created an array of competing new social identities, not always to be pinpointed easily. In this atmosphere, the fall of Communism began to be seen as a distant event, with less and less bearing on the present. There were other things to be worried about, many people in former Communist countries began to think and feel – and they were probably right. As if this was not enough, on top came the worsening geopolitical situation in Europe and the world, combined with economic, migration and health crises. Thus thirty years after the fall of the Berlin Wall a stage was set for what would come to be known as 'illiberal Europe', with its geographic centre seen as located in Eastern Europe. Eastern Europe was finally placed at the centre of (unwanted) attention.

The Rule of Law:
Illiberal Europe?

The EU enlargement of 2004, which brought into the Union eight countries from Central Europe (and two from Europe's South) was the very culmination of a period that began with the fall of the Berlin Wall and was hailed as the end of history. (Bulgaria and Romania followed in 2007.) During this quarter of a century, Europe (and the world) saw the end of Communism in Europe (though not globally), the (re) creation of (new) independent states, and their accession to the EU and NATO. This was the feast of Europe's idealism, a victory for the region, a window of opportunity well earned, but also quite unique and rare in international relations.

But already in 2001 came the wake-up call of 9/11, a sign that this historic window of opportunity was closing. The attack on the Twin Towers had a global impact, though the alarm clock was set for the West in particular. After the invasion of the Taliban's Afghanistan in 2001, which had a quite clear rationale, the US invaded Iraq in March of 2003 for reasons not totally understood and poorly linked to the terrorist threat, leading to opposition from various corners. However in Central Europe, Poland joined the Iraq military campaign, morally supported by the wider so-called 'Coalition of the Willing', which included a number of other Central European countries who thus seized the opportunity of boosting their chances of NATO membership.

The invasion of Iraq was another milestone announcing that the velvet era in international relations was coming to an end, an era in which empires collapsed with little collateral damage, regimes swiftly changed and new small states were, almost without objections, allowed to come into existence. Now it was again the Martian vision of the world that was gaining traction. Yet this view of the world was not just simplistic and brutal. It also included a (conservative or liberal) belief in classic human freedom as something universal, attainable by all. Therefore, it was not only the Central Europeans that were worthy of a regime change to free themselves of Communist oppression: in the Middle East, Arab peoples also deserved better than to be ruled by ruthless dictators, even if freeing them needed to be done by force. It was not difficult to convince Central Europeans to support this way of thinking and even to join the American military campaign, although they must have been aware of the naivety of the belief that their path to democracy could be replicated in a completely different social setting, where dictators appeared to be the best guardians of delicate balances between peoples and religious factions, and the Enlightenment was almost unheard of.

On the other side of Eastern Europe, Putin's reading of the aftermath of the invasion of Iraq was different, and, in a certain way, definitely more realistic. For him, the military campaign was a proof that the 'West's self-proclaimed pursuit of democracy and freedom only brings instability and suffering in its wake.'[104] This analysis by the Russian leader is not important in as much as it is true, but more to the extent in

104. Rachman, G, *The Age of the Strongman*, Bodley Head, London, p. 32.

which it is false, namely, the implication that the West should sit idle and not try to promote its values. In the eyes of Putin, his own understanding of events was confirmed by the 2003 Rose Revolution in Georgia, marking a pro-Western turn, and a similar Orange Revolution in Ukraine in 2004: instability came dangerously close to Russia's front yard.

Central Europe's hasty embrace of the US approach was certainly not welcome in France and the rest of the Continent, except with some conservative governments. And while everyone was aware of the largely opportunistic nature of such a position on the part of Central European governments, there began to emerge a new gap, previously unknown, between Europe's East and West. On the one side of this gap was Western Europe, for a long time now at peace, enjoying an unparalleled level of prosperity created by the post-war socio-economic consensus of the mainstream political forces of left and right, based on the narrative of World War II as a great conflict between liberal thought and Fascism. In this narrative, Communism (if you discount the Soviet contribution in the war itself) had only a side role; it was seen more as an aberration of liberal democracy, rather than its true opponent. After all, there was no lack of admirers of the Soviet Union and Communist ideas in post-war Europe, not only among extremist leftist organisations like *Brigate Rosse* in Italy or *Baader-Meinhof-Gruppe* in Germany. In any event, Communism was believed to be won over and gone with the fall of the Berlin Wall. There was no need to be worried about it anymore. The menace of the revolution, a source of such great concern for the Western leaders during the interwar years, and the Soviet atomic threat, a source of post-World War II worries, were now gone. And while the memory of World War II was thus fading away, and so was (an important part of) the rationale it provided for the existence of the European Union, the liberal narrative took a twist, being further deepened by the emergence of post-modern thought that pushed the idea of an autonomous individual to the very limits. Critical race, gender and other related theories have become the flagship ideas of the Western left, rather than the condition of the working classes, now almost extinct in a de-industrialised West.

On the other hand, out there in the East, there were peoples, so far largely unknown, that should return to Europe, should adopt the entire canon of the West, and should begin to copy the West. Their historical experience was of limited interest, at times too graphic and brutal for elevated circles or too complex for an ordinary Western voter to understand. And these Easterns then suddenly departed from Europe's way (together with Prime Minister Tony Blair) on a trip with those conservative Americans, as if too naive to understand that it was all about oil and America's lack of sophistication in international affairs. This was the impression at least in the upper circles of Europe's core nations.

In fact, this more sophisticated Europe was right. The invasion of Iraq was an ill-conceived and poorly justified enterprise, as America would acknowledge later. True, a brutal dictator was gone, but the country and the region was thrown out of balance, into years of conflict, civil strife and misery, with only Iran seeming to profit from it.

However, by the outbreak of the 2008 economic crisis, the Iraq episode was almost forgotten. Central Europe was then hit hard by the crisis, with the exception of Poland, which maintained growth due to the size of its domestic market, reliance on local currency and fairly healthy banks. (This Polish exception should not be forgotten, as it provides part of the rationale for later developments.) The Baltic states,

Bulgaria, Romania and Hungary had the hardest times. They were more dependent on foreign investments and were heavily exposed to Scandinavian and Austrian banks. (In the Baltics, banks were also exposed to extensive Russian attempts at money laundering.) Eventually, the banking sector was rescued by international financial institutions, and once growth resumed in Germany, the region's economies also recovered. The Czech Republic (with solid banks and relatively strong manufacturing), Slovenia and Slovakia managed the crisis a bit better.

It is important to note these differences, but also the fact that Central Europe still performed better than the European South. And it was on the latter that the eyes of Central Europeans were focused at the time, on Greece in particular. (There were some degrading statements about Greece also by Central Europeans and, in 2015, the Slovenian finance minister allegedly suggested that Greece should leave the Eurozone – imagine the furore by Greeks, being told something like that by an Eastern European.) They were carefully looking at the attitude of Europe's north to these countries, which was very telling: concrete gestures of solidarity with Greece (and other countries in financial distress) eventually came, but after some wrangling and dragging of feet, and at a high price. The message that has been taken by Eastern Europeans was that there were limits to European solidarity.

In the meantime and in the shadow of European economic woes, Putin intervened militarily in Georgia in 2008, effectively enabling the creation of two breakaway entities within that country. The Russian leader calculated well that he could easily go that far, and his hopes were confirmed by only mild reactions from the West. But this only further increased the concerns of many Central Europeans.

Soon after, there was again turmoil in the Arab world. In December 2010 the so-called Arab Spring set off in Tunisia and, in early 2011, protests erupted across the Middle East, triggered by a mixture of autocratic rule and oppression, corruption, and the dire economic and social situation. (Religion played a role too – something that continues to be under-explored, perhaps simply because Western secularism has made its citizens ignorant about religion.) In a handful of countries (Tunisia, Morocco, Algeria) these protests resulted in minor concessions by those in power. But in some the consequences were devastating. In Egypt, Hosni Mubarak was toppled and the leader of the Muslim Brotherhood, Mohamed Morsi, became President in 2012 before he was removed by the army the following year. In Libya, another tyrant, Muammar Gadaffi was overthrown with indirect assistance from a France-initiated, multinational UN force, but today the country is still divided into areas controlled by different factions and serves as a gatekeeper or as a springboard for African migrants to Europe, at times in an embarrassing way for Europe. Even worse was the well-known fate of Syria.

It soon became obvious that it was not possible to replicate what had happened in Central Europe in the Arab world and that perhaps it should not even have been attempted. And not only that. The failed Arab Spring and the resulting ongoing civil strife, aided by the global availability of social media and even climate change, led to a surge of migrants.

The time of velvet revolutions was over – or so it seemed. Even in Europe's immediate vicinity like Georgia and Ukraine, where another revolution, the so-called Maidan Uprising of 2013, aimed to set the country on a pro-European path. This too, however, was followed by Russian intervention and annexation of the Crimea peninsula in 2014 (and later by even more direct aggression in February 2022). So the embrace of liberal democracy was difficult not only in the Middle East, but on Europe's periphery too, as it seemed to stand in the way of Putin's Russia and his way of thinking. Russia was more and more resembling the Soviet Union – something Putin actually wanted, as his grievances over the collapse of the socialist empire suggest. Events in Belarus in 2020 were another reminder that, what, in the first part of this book, I termed 'Eastern Europe proper', would also not have the same easy way to democracy and full sovereignty as Central Europe: Russia would not let them slip easily out of the Soviet orbit, now being remade by Putin. The window, let open by Gorbachev, was closing indeed and that was the message to the democrats (and, as encouragement, to autocrats too) around the world. After all, Russians themselves could get ideas, should democratic movements in neighbouring countries actually succeed.

The leaders in Central Europe were aware of all that; they also noted that in the US, both Donald Trump's Republicans and the Democrats of Joe Biden do not believe in regime change anymore, at least not in an engineered one. But they still feared Putin's Russia – for a good reason, as demonstrated in Georgia, Ukraine and even Syria.

There was also another, much more subtle message from these developments, including one from the economic crisis that Central Europeans took with them: that they are much more on their own, both in the world and within the EU. And that Western liberal democracy has given up when faced with authoritarian regimes in the Middle East and perhaps also in the case of Eastern Europe. This perceived weakness of Europe and its liberal democracy, the lack of will to sacrifice for its professed values, portrayed, in the eyes of Central Europe, a picture of Western Europe that is strong on individual rights and liberties, and on safeguarding a high level of living standards at home, but weak when trying to uphold these values outside its own territory. Furthermore, the focus of the societies in the West has not been anymore on political and basic human rights (so important for newly emerged democracies, but in the West now taken for granted), but increasingly on the intimate world of an atomised individual, his rights and liberties, however peculiar, specific and distinct, put high on the altar of the new secular religion, whose high priests reside not anymore in the now abandoned churches, but in a dense network of independent institutions, arts and NGOs. This was now another world – Charles Taylor's secular age.

A look at the Atlas of European Values[105] confirms this growing gap between the two halves of Europe – and the changed character of Western Europe. Ethically sensitive or philosophically relevant issues like religion and God, race and nationality, immigration, homosexuality and family and abortion, trust, equality, the death penalty, etc. show – usually though not always – a markedly different pattern of popular opinion in Central and Eastern Europe, compared with the West. (There are, however, also cases when the CEE pattern is similar to the South European one, and there are also differences in public opinion among the three tiers of Eastern Europe.)

What is important here is the realisation that this post-modern, 'woke' Europe was not anymore the one that Central Europeans thought they were subscribing to in the early 1990s, the one with classic liberal values and still some appreciation for Christian identity, the one known to those conservative

---

105. https://www.atlasofeuropeanvalues.eu/

EU-enthusiasts. No, it became a Europe unsure of its identity, repudiating the last remaining signs of its Christian and even Humanistic and classical liberal roots for the sake of greater inclusivity in an increasingly diverse society: '... suddenly, Poles have discovered that Western "normality" means secularism, multiculturalism and gay marriage.'[106] These were values and concepts that were, at best, of only secondary interest in Central Europe. Moreover, the way they were promoted caused fear that they want to replace conservative values appreciated in the region and change the identity of Europe as a whole. Furthermore, this perceived lack of a clear European identity (or simply the advent of a new identity) opened the window wide not only to various conspiracy theories, but also to radical and extreme positions. It also offered a suitable explanation of political developments, statements and European Parliament declarations that Eastern Europeans found it difficult to subscribe to. In fact, in the view of many in Central Europe, repeated difficulties with the European constitution, the Conference on the Future of Europe, and the European Commission's portfolio for the European way of life were proof of Europe being unsure about what it is and what it stands for. E.g., the Letter of Intent, a policy document accompanying the EU State of the Union 2022 document, lists under the heading of 'Promoting our European Way of Life' the following items: mental health, recognition of qualifications, digitalisation of travel documents, facilitation of travel, combating child sexual abuse and cybersecurity skills academy. These are hardly attributes of a distinct culture or way of life.[107]

---

106. Krastev, I, Holmes, S, *The Light that Failed*, Allen Lane, 2019, p. 52.
107. https://state-of-the-union.ec.europa.eu/system/files/2022-09/SOTEU_ 2022_Letter_of_Intent_EN_0.pdf

Krastev, probably the leading thinker on these issues in Central Europe, seems to share the concern when he talks about the time *after Europe* in which 'Europe is suffering from an identity crisis in which its Christian and Enlightenment legacies are no longer secure'.[108] It is important to note that he does not refer only to Christianity (which Orbán could do too), but also to Enlightenment: it is not just about the Christian heritage – to which so many in the liberal West may be averse – but classic liberalism is in decline too. However, this identity crisis seems to worry – rightfully so – the advocates of liberal democracy when it comes to (right-wing or conservative) populism in Eastern Europe, but less so when faced with a radical liberal or leftist, post-modern or 'woke' agenda in the West. In their view, the danger to liberal democracy comes from the socially conservative side only.

The stage was thus set – in the most inconvenient way possible – for the next scene, that of the mass arrival in 2015-16 of migrants, largely Syrians from Turkey, coming via Greece, and from there to Western Europe, through the Balkans or via Hungary. There, Prime Minister Viktor Orbán insisted on the EU asylum and migration rule-book, pointing out that the situation was untenable, and seizing the opportunity to sound the alarm about the impending overflow of Europe by Muslim migrants. Islamic terrorism that shook Europe in the early 2000s (the Madrid 2004 and London 2005 bombings) and in particular attacks after 2014 that came as one of the (indirect) consequences of the invasion of Iraq and civil strife in the wider Middle East, as well as a result of failed integration of radicalised individuals, were also used as a useful argument that these migrants, especially the young men among them, represent a security

---

108. Krastev, I, *After Europe*, University of Pennsylvania Press, 2017, p. 9.

threat for Europe. Hungary and most of the rest of Central Europe was taken aback by the average Western European's apparent complete ignorance of the cultural challenge that such masses of devout or outright radicalised Muslims represent. As a result, chaotic and unpleasant scenes could be seen in Hungary of migrants not being welcome, which inspired Angela Merkel to suspend the EU legislation and accept migrants *en masse,* while Hungary embarked on building a new fence, resembling a wall, which was only recently brought down.

Chancellor Merkel was widely praised for her actions abroad and at home – except in the former Eastern Germany. While media and analysts did notice different reactions in this part of Germany, few took the trouble of looking under the surface of the alleged xenophobia of the former Communist lands. (In that respect, the former DDR offered an excellent living laboratory.) These people seemed just so selfish and ungrateful. Together with Central European countries, which resisted the plan for distribution of the migrants among EU countries, they were named and shamed for their alleged lack of sympathy for those in need of refuge. They were reminded how the West took care of those fleeing over the Iron Curtain during the Communist years. In this picture, Hungary and Poland stood out, seeing the arrival of masses of many young males (after the first wave of mainly women, children and families) foremost as a security issue and, what was most controversial and difficult to understand in the West, as a threat to Christian nations of Europe and their way of life. The truth was that by then, few in the West cared about Christian tradition. And even those that did, thought that – much to the annoyance of Eastern Europe – it was precisely this Christian tradition that required nothing less than a warm welcome of the migrants.

On the surface, the idea of redistribution of refugees/

migrants across Europe seemed noble and reasonable: Greece, Malta and Italy had been for a very long time unfairly carrying the bulk of the burden of migration, due to an unworkable EU rule requiring the country of the first entry to process the refugee. However, in practice it became evident that it was migrants who – now empowered, also through social media, by international conventions and Western sense of individual rights – were determined not to accept the first entry rule and wanted to have a final destination of their own choice. Their expectations of what they are entitled to also run high. In addition, the UN-wide 1951 Refugee Convention, invoked also during this mass wave, put considerable pressure on recipient countries. Many governments (loudly or tacitly) felt that the Convention may have worked out in a post-World War II setting, where it was mostly about European refugees seeking safe havens, but was difficult to implement in conditions of large-scale immigration from outside Europe, often facilitated by human traffickers or third-state actors.

And then there was the cultural element – the will to generously accept masses of migrants or refugees seemed to be in tune with the Western idea of multicultural society, an idea largely unknown or at least untested in culturally much more homogenous Eastern European countries.

Western Europe faced the first modern challenges in the field of migration at the end of the nineteenth century (German annexation of Alsace, Polish workers, French 'integration' of the Basques and Bretons) and with the labour needs after World War I.[109] This need became even more acute after World

109. For a historical account of migrations in Europe see Chin, R, *The Crisis of Multiculturalism in Europe: A History*, Princeton University Press, 2017. A brief summary of the relevant passages of this book is provided on the following pages.

War II, when a new element emerged, especially for Great Britain, France and the Netherlands – the arrival of people from their former colonies. For France, the most difficult case was Algeria, as Algerians were in fact its citizens or at least enjoyed the freedom of settlement in France. The same was true for British colonies in the Caribbean and India, and Dutch possessions in Indonesia. All of these countries primarily wanted to get labour from Europe, but – firstly as part of efforts to preserve overseas possessions and then in the process of decolonisation – they also had to agree to the arrival of non-European workers.

There was a significant complication in France, where Algerian workers were often seen as agents of the Algerian struggle for independence; the French public increasingly perceived them as a violent threat to France due to the terrorist acts during the 1960s. Some of the Indonesian immigrants also brought political divisions to the new-old homeland of the Netherlands. Nevertheless, employers' desire for cheap labour did not wane in France or elsewhere until the oil crisis in the early 1970s. It was during this period that we could see the beginnings of the first conflicts between the indigenous population of Western Europe and non-European immigrants.[110] By then, however, all these countries began to look for legal and other ways to curb the arrival of (no longer economically necessary) migrant workers or even encouraged them to return home. Welcome reasons for this were also the developments in the European Union and the principle of free movement of workers within it, which enabled workers from the Union's Mediterranean countries to work in the

---

110. Chin, R, *The Crisis of Multiculturalism in Europe: A History*, Princeton Univeristy Press, 2017, p. 139.

West and the North. At the time, though, the number of non-European workers (and their family members whose arrival was explicitly or tacitly allowed by the countries mentioned) had already grown so much that they had become a social problem, even if countries such as Germany have long insisted that they are just guest workers and not real immigrants.

Aware of the tragic experience of Nazism (and also because of their bad consciences about it), post-war European governments avoided racist undertones in their efforts to curb non-European immigration. They based their new policy on the risk to public order and peace, and only later on the incompatibility of cultures – Chin speaks of 'cultural nationalism'[111] adopted by both left and right, partly due to movements such as Le Pen's party in France. It was France that went through long and wide public debates in the 1980s, trying to redefine what it means to be French; most of these discussions agreed on the need for a common language, culture, civic values and integration, which must not weaken the national identity – that is, by emphasising the integration of immigrants but also their assimilation. In the UK and Germany, a little more room was left for cultural pluralism.

According to Chin, a decisive milestone in the approach to immigrant policy in Western Europe came with the publication of *The Satanic Verses* by Salman Rushdie in 1988. In Britain, Muslims availed themselves of democratic means to prevent the publication of this book, which, in their view, severely offended their religious sentiments. However, when the Iranian ayatollah became involved in this European story with a deadly fatwa against Rushdie, the perception in British (and other Western societies) changed: the opposition to the book became a

---

111. Chin, p. 140.

problem of a supposedly monolithic, unchanging world Muslim community incapable of accepting the European principle of freedom of speech and not fully prepared to give up violence. (Rushdie was actually stabbed and severely wounded in an attack in the United States in August 2022.) From *The Satanic Verses*, attention has thus shifted to the Muslim community in Europe, to their apparently awkward religion being at odds with the liberal values of British and other European cultures: similarly, Turkish culture in West Germany and Algerian in France were increasingly seen as problematic.[112]

It is significant that these developments (accidentally) coincided with the fall of the Iron Curtain and the 'return' of former European communist countries to the imagined community of 'Europe'. Namely, this coincidence only further strengthened Western confidence both towards non-European immigrants as well as now former 'Eastern' Europeans. The war in what was Yugoslavia, with its ethnic and religious undertones, also aroused a degree of cultural fear.

The issue of the (in)compatible culture of European Muslims (and other non-Western people) thus called into question the hitherto considerable support for the concept of multiculturalism. There is certainly some confusion as to the meaning of this word: it could be simply a factual description of the existence of different cultural communities in a society, or of government policies to address related issues. Or, as some would claim, an ideology that would see an inherent moral quality in the mere existence of such a community and therefore something that needs to be actively encouraged.

But whatever the meaning, multiculturalism was soon to be pronounced dead in Europe. Chancellor Merkel in 2010 stated,

---

112. Chin, p. 187 – 188.

with some regret, that multiculturalism 'failed utterly' and that it was an illusion to believe that the Germans and foreign workers could 'live happily side by side', although she also recognised that Islam was now a part of German culture.[113]

The situation was similar in other countries. When I came to the Netherlands as a diplomat in 2009, the country had already had a difficult migration experience and had more or less lost faith in multiculturalism. In November 2004, a young Muslim man in Amsterdam brutally murdered a Dutch film director Theo van Gogh (coincidentally related to the famous painter), in revenge for van Gogh's film, critical of Islam and made in collaboration with Ayaan Hersi Ali, a Somali-born Dutch who became an atheist and a vocal critic of Islam. In his book *Murder in Amsterdam*, Dutch historian and writer Ian Buruma explored the reasons that led to such a tragic showdown between an immigrant and an ethnic Dutchman. He was critical of Dutch tolerance of immigrants: 'The tolerance of other cultures, often barely understood, that spread with new waves of migration, was sometimes just that – tolerance – and sometimes sheer indifference, bred by a lack of confidence in values and institutions that needed to be defended.'[114] Buruma described Dutch society at the time as 'post-multi-cult confusion' associated with Dutch feelings of guilt from World War II (some believe that the Netherlands did not do enough at the time to defend its Jews) and the negative attitudes towards Moroccan and Turkish guest workers. He sums up the words of Muhammad, the later murderer of Theo van Gogh, that 'Holland would be the cradle of a religious revolution, made possible by

---

113. https://www.theguardian.com/world/2010/oct/17/angela-merkel-germany-multiculturalism-failures
114. Buruma, I, *Murder in Amsterdam*, Atlantic Books, 2006, p. 34.

precisely those political liberties that Mohammad affected to despise.'[115]

Among the thinkers mentioned by Buruma in his book is the Dutch sociologist Paul Scheffer, who in 2007 published the influential book *Immigrant Nations*. It analyses in detail the phenomenon of immigration from other cultures, both from the point of view of immigrants and native residents. His central idea is that both groups need to be subjected to critical reflection. Scheffer advocates a new definition of citizenship based on history and culture, taking into account the contribution of immigrants: 'Citizenship is all about a consciousness that something came before us and something will come after us.'[116] He calls for the introduction of citizenship rituals, for more attention in the school system to history and law, and for a canon of national history. In the process of integration, the immigrant must, in his view, acquire a range of knowledge and skills. Above all, integration is about 'the willingness to be part of society', and this inevitably means re-evaluating the tradition brought from elsewhere, says Scheffer. At the same time, integration requires an environment in which migrants and their children feel invited to participate in society. He concludes that multiculturalism was naive and wrong: 'Multiculturalism offered an answer that contained no obligation when it said that it has become meaningless to talk about "us" because society is a collection of subcultures ... A new "we" is needed.'[117] And further: 'Without "us", without an imagined community, there will be no shared responsibility for the changing destiny of society.'[118] He stresses that the nation

---

115. Buruma, p. 217.

116. Scheffer, P, *Immigrant Nations*, Polity Press, 2011, p. 305.

117. Scheffer, p. 297.

118. Scheffer, p. 298. Scheffer uses the term 'imagined community', as developed by Benedict Anderson in his 1983 book with the same title.

state is still an important institution for the identification of individuals, even if citizenship of the European Union offers at least a temporary option to facilitate the integration of immigrants. (Chin's reasoning is similar. She believes that in dealing with the integration of immigrants, 'we cannot simply return to some originalist conception of Enlightenment individualism' nor 'can we cling to a blind, unreconstructed celebration of pluralism and cultural relativism'.[119])

Scheffer also wonders why there have been problems with integration on the part of the host society. He notes that part of the responsibility also lies with the social-liberal society and even the sexual revolution, which 'brought not only freedom but also new forms of dependence',[120] making reference to the French writer Michel Houellebecq. Radical individualism destroys the family and reduces the citizen to a consumer. One can find a similar argument about sexuality (she talks about 'sexual democracy'[121]) in Chin's book – and there is certainly no lack of things sexual in works by Houellebecq!

It should then not come as a surprise that '[n]owhere does the cultural war in Central and Eastern Europe rage more fiercely, in fact, than it does around sex education in schools.'[122] This centrality of cultural and ethical issues, even most intimate ones, is key to understanding the root causes of 'illiberal Europe' and culture wars in the Europe of today. It resonates with the abortion legislation in Poland and LGBT themes in education in Hungary – but also, as we continue to witness, in the United States. We should not forget that either.

---

119. Chin, p. 302.
120. Scheffer, p. 300.
121. Chin, p. 228 – 236.
122. Krastev, I, Holmes, S, p. 53.

I read Scheffer's work at a time when (in 2012, four years before Brexit) the issue of workers from the new member states of the European Union, especially Poland and the Baltic States, was becoming more acute in the Netherlands. They simply started to bother some Dutch people: a Dutchman openly told me that he felt threatened when he found himself in a shop alone with, say, five Poles. Even politics did not always know how to show respect for them. The state still divided people into indigenous and non-indigenous in official statistics.

That year the right-wing populist PVV party of Geert Wilders launched a website *Meldpunt Midden en Oost Europeanen* designed to be a place for online complaints against nationals from Central and Eastern Europe living and working in the Netherlands. Prime Minister Mark Rutte, whose government relied on tacit support from the PVV, refused to unambiguously condemn the campaign. I was in a group of ten Central European ambassadors that requested a meeting with the then foreign minister Rosenthal. During the meeting, I stressed that we should counter populism wherever it appears and that it is therefore important for the government to speak up about European values. Nothing came as a result of the meeting. But this example – years before the migration crisis of 2015, in which it was Eastern Europe that was not a welcoming host – showed the centrality of the migration issues, and the underlying cultural and philosophical questions. It also showed that populism and xenophobia are not limited to former Communist lands. They have been a part and parcel of society in France (Le Pen's RN and Mélenchon's La France Insoumise – as the election of 2022 showed), the Netherlands (Geert Wilders and perhaps even more the Forum for Democracy), Italy (Forza Italia, Lega and increasingly the Brothers of Italy), Sweden (Sweden Democrats), Austria

(Freedom Party) and Germany (AdF and Die Linke), not to mention the United States. Also, Gideon Rachman in his book on 'strongmen' around the world unashamedly lists Boris Johnson, former UK Prime Minister, among the likes of Putin, Erdogan, Xi Jinping, Modi, Orbán, Kaczyński, Trump and Duterte, saying that 'in a very English way, he had introduced important elements of the strongman style of politics into Britain. He had shown a willingness to break both domestic and international law. He had demonised opponents as elitist enemies of the people.' In Rachman's view, '[g]iven Britain's position as one of the world's oldest democracies, the election of a populist rule-breaker as UK Prime Minister marked a significant shift in European and world politics.'[123] Anne Applebaum affirms too that this is not an Eastern European problem only, stressing that populism in Eastern Europe is a phenomenon of the last decade.[124]

To be fair, Western European countries are well equipped to face these political movements with an array of long-established institutions, well-developed and plural civil society organisations and quality independent media. All these do not have the same strength and tradition in Eastern Europe, so the danger to the social fabric is much greater. Still, the fact that in the West such political parties have been thriving despite this array of institutions is no less troubling. In fact, it raises doubts about their strength too.

In all these (and other) countries the increasingly weak political mainstream has been fighting hard to fend off

---

123. Rachman, G, *The Age of the Strongman: How the Cult of the Leader Threatens Democracy around the World*, The Bodley Head, London 2022, pp. 116 – 117.
124. Applebaum, A, *Twilight of Democracy: The Seductive Lure of Authoritarianism*, Doubleday, 2020, p. 56.

populism and an anti-immigration stance or even the prospect of the return of fascism. This long-term decline of traditional parties is part of the reason why 'there will be room on the political spectrum for anti-establishment populists and hard-line nationalists for many years to come.'[125] What is worrying is that in most cases, these populist and extremist parties are no longer obscure, fringe parties that ordinary decent people avoid but organisations that enjoy considerable popular support and have realistic chances of coming to power, at least at regional level. In some instances, otherwise mainstream parties have adopted migration and integration policies that raise eyebrows. For example, Social-Democrats in Denmark have, at least at regional level, broken the taboo of not forming coalitions with radical parties. This development shows that globalisation, de-industrialisation, large-scale immigration, and the failure of liberal democracy to deliver fast and effective solutions to these challenges have aroused discontented individuals on both the left and the right of the political spectrum. They were further persuaded by excessive political correctness and an aggressive 'woke' culture, the crusade of the cancel culture and simply by the denial of the existence of problems, together with the blaming and shaming of all those who draw attention to them.

Among these challenges, the migration issue had a prominent place, as it increased the feeling of insecurity. As early as 2007, Scheffer wondered whether the (already mentioned) 1951 United Nations Convention on Refugees was still suitable for a period of mass refugee movements. Distinguished migration experts Alexander Betts and Paul Collier expressed similar

---

125. Barber, T, 'One step forwards, two steps back for Europe's hard right', *Financial Times*, 30 April 2022.

doubts about this convention in their high-profile book *Refuge*. They point out that the 1951 Convention was a product of its time and space, quickly prepared for the international community, at the initiative of the United States, to face the movements that took place at the start of the Cold War. The convention defined a refugee as a person who left his or her own country due to a 'reasonable fear of persecution' based on race, religion, nationality, membership of a social group, or political option. The document was designed to be used until the end of 1953, it applied only to persons who became refugees as a result of events before 1951, and was geographically limited to Europe. The 1967 Protocol removed this geographical restriction, which the authors see as an expression of hasty Eurocentrism.[126] In addition, in their view, the 1951 Convention did not clearly answer the questions of whom, how and where to protect. Namely, modern migrations or even modern refugees are by no means (only) the result of classical persecution (as defined above), but are fleeing for survival or because their countries of origin have disintegrated or failed, or even because of the effects of climate change. The two authors are particularly critical of the established model of refugee camps, as they often become a lasting solution to keeping refugees away from the countries that fund them.[127]

The migration wave of 2015, triggered also by Russia's military intervention in Syria's civil war, led to more than 4 million Syrians fleeing to neighbouring Jordan, Turkey and Lebanon. These – not exactly rich countries – have been exposed to an extraordinary burden, which neither the OECD (Organisation for Economic Cooperation and Development)

---

126. Betts, A, Collier, P, *Refuge: Transforming a Broken Refugee System*, Penguin Books, 2018, p. 36 – 39.
127. Ibid., p. 42 – 60.

members nor their rich Arab OPEC (Organisation of the Petroleum Exporting Countries) neighbours have been able or willing to finance. The UNHCR (United Nations High Commission for Refugees) has provided refugees in these countries with relative security, food and shelter, but they still faced unemployment without any real prospects. Many soon became aware of the proximity of the 'Greek Lampedusa' – the island of Lesbos, from where continental Europe can be reached.

In August 2015, the Syrian regime's military position deteriorated again, so Russia had to come to the rescue. Germany's decision to open the door to refugees even beyond the provisions of the common European migration system was, inadvertently, an additional impetus to the Syrian population in areas where Assad was aided by the Russian military. Betts and Collier suggest that the Russian president actually had his reasons for encouraging such an exodus to Germany. Migrations can indeed be misused as a geopolitical and/or international security tool.

The migration wave of 2015/16 was really something special, a novelty and something inconceivable even for diplomats and consular officials. For years, from their first consular training, diplomats have been instilled with the idea of respecting strict EU rules related to security and sovereignty, and with the basic postulates that every person from a country with a visa requirement is subject to security and migration checks. Diplomats (and border police officers) could only hold their breath as countries, in the midst of the migration crisis in the autumn and winter of 2015, allowed people to cross their borders not only without pre-obtained visas, but often even without any identification and without knowing where they were heading to.

So history did not end, after all. It was being created in a most challenging way. There was no time for complacency anymore:[128] the Russian annexation of Crimea (apparently a prelude for 2022's full-scale invasion), the 2015 refugee crisis, Brexit in 2016 and Trump in America attested to that. Something had to be done. Chancellor Merkel struck a deal with Turkey, 'a slightly dirty deal that arguably replicated some of the controls of freedom of movement demanded by the likes of Orbán, without fully acknowledging it.'[129] The gates of Europe were open to prove its high values. Germans, in particular, still offered a noble example of a welcoming society.

Hungary and the rest of Central Europe too felt that the end of history was nowhere near, even if their way of thinking was different. First, there was an objection to the procedure by which the decision on redistribution was taken within the EU. (It was later challenged unsuccessfully in the EU court, though the discussion on widening the scope of the so-called quality majority vote continues.) There was also a practical argument: how on earth could one prevent migrants or refugees from leaving, at the earliest opportunity, say, Slovakia, and heading for Germany or Sweden. In the eyes of Central Europeans, Europe appeared naive, weak, unable to deal with the migration wave, certainly unable to stop it and to effectively police its borders. This must have, they reckoned, something to do with Western Europe's philosophical underpinning: 'Central Europe's fearmongering populists interpreted the refugee crisis as a conclusive evidence that liberalism has weakened the capacity of nations to defend themselves in a

---

128. Rachman, G, *The Age of the Strongman*, Bodley Head, London, p. 193.
129. Ibid., p. 195.

hostile world.'[130] In another place, Krastev concludes: 'It was liberalism's failure to address the migration problem, rather than economic crisis or rising inequality, that explains the public turn against it.'[131]

But more important, even if much more tacit, was, as already suggested, the argument of not being ready for culturally different or distant migrants. For sure, former Eastern bloc nations had, even during the Communist time, some contact with comrades from friendly third-world countries. But these were mostly students and experts on a mission of limited duration. (An interesting exception is the Vietnamese community in the Czech Republic whose origin lies in the arrival of substantial numbers of guest workers.) The fact that Eastern Europe does not have a colonial experience also means that it 'thus lacks a sense of guilt, but it also lacks a shared fate that often accompanies colonial encounters.'[132]

It was not only xenophobia, but genuine concern about how Central Europe could possibly succeed where the likes of the Netherlands, Germany and Sweden had failed. In April 2022, the Swedish Social Democratic Prime Minister conceded what others had been observing for a long time: that its integration policies have failed.[133] This became the key topic of the general elections that same year which propelled the Sweden Democrats to the position of a kingmaker of the new government. (To be fair, there is also a failure of Eastern Europe itself to deal with its own Roma population,[134] who are not immigrants.) And there

---

130. Krastev, I, Holmes, S, *The Light that Failed*, Allan Lane, 2019, p. 34.
131. Krastev, I, *After Europe*, p. 25.
132. Ibid., p. 55.
133. https://www.reuters.com/world/europe/swedish-pm-says-integration-immigrants-has-failed-fueled-gang-crime-2022-04-28/ (retrieved on 13 June 2022)
134. Krastev, I, *After Europe*, p. 54.

was probably also a feeling that accommodating and integrating large numbers of migrants would take a toll on Central Europe's race to catch up with Western Europe.

In any event, the region's reaction to the refugee crisis cemented a view of it as an alien, xenophobic and anti-immigrant, socially conservative part of Europe – 'illiberal Europe', an image that will have been only partially corrected with the overwhelming welcome given to millions of war refugees from Ukraine in 2022, during a migrant wave much bigger than the one of 2015-2016. But not even this has taken away the negative image of illiberal Europe.

Ivan Krastev, probably one of the region's best analysts, cites possible explanations for Eastern fear about migrants. One of them is depopulation (which hit Bulgaria, Romania and the Baltics in particular), as a result of free movement of labour. According to Krastev, the fear of depopulation has been substituted with the fear of (Muslim) foreigners. Related to it is the experience of these same Central European expats, who in the West often end up living in the same neighbourhoods as Muslims, and therefore want to disassociate from them. But most importantly, '[t]he refugee crisis has made it clear that Eastern Europe views the very cosmopolitan values on which the European Union is based as a threat, while for many in the West it is precisely those cosmopolitan values that are at the core of the new European identity.[135] [...] The resistance of liberals to conceding any negative effects of migration has triggered the anti-establishment (and particularly anti-mainstream media) reaction that is convulsing political life in democracies in so many places today.'[136] How exactly did

---

135. Krastev, I, *After Europe*, p. 47.
136. Ibid., p. 50.

we come to that? Let's look at the Hungarian and Polish case first.

Paul Lendvai is an Austrian journalist of Hungarian descent, a Social Democrat who fled to Austria after the suppression of the Hungarian uprising in 1956. In his book *Orbán: Europe's New Strongman*, he does not skimp on criticism of the Hungarian Prime Minister and describes with passion and concern for his native country Orbán's rise to what is now seen as a near-total power, a capture of the state.

Interestingly enough and as Lendvai points out, nothing in Orbán's childhood indicated his later anti-communist mood; the family was apparently a conformist one. A bold move, however, was the founding of Fidesz in 1988 at a student college in Budapest. Orbán's then student colleagues are still his closest allies, and almost without exception they come from very modest rural circles, not liberal or leftist Budapest elites, who looked down on them – an experience that has supposedly left a strong mark on Orbán and has dictated his later political credo.[137]

The party was successful in the first democratic election (Orbán was the first to publicly call for the withdrawal of Soviet troops from Hungary at a major rally – it was this that gave him prominence), but was defeated in the following elections in 1994. Hungary then came to be ruled by a coalition of the former communist Socialist party ('a snake pit of old Communists and left wing careerists posing as Social Democrats'[138]) and the new Free Democrats party. But a year later, Orbán drove his hitherto liberal (sometimes even anti-church) Fidesz to the right and won his first term as Prime Minister in 1998. The results of his tenure were a significant

---

137. Lendvai, P, *Orbán: Europe's New Strongman*, Oxford University Press, 2017, p. 11 and 21.
138. Ibid., p. 74.

statutory and public sector wage increase and generous incentives for private housing, unsupported by the state of public finances – all these laid the foundations for Hungary's economic debacle in 2002-2010, for which, however, the subsequent coalition of Socialists and Free Democrats would be mostly responsible.[139]

The government of Socialist Prime Minister Medgyessy was then overthrown in 2002 following the publication of a news piece in an opposition newspaper, claiming that he had been an agent of the Communist Secret Police. He was succeeded by Mr Gyurcsany, considered by Lendvai to be Hungary's 'most capable, controversial and unpredictable (and certainly richest) politician on the left',[140] who managed to successfully hide the real economic situation and widespread corruption up until autumn 2006. That year a secretly recorded closed-door discussion by Gyurcsany went on air in which the Prime Minister bluntly admitted that the government had been lying to the public for some time and had also not done anything right in the same period.

This brought Orbán back to power in the April 2010 elections in which Fidesz alone gained a two-thirds majority, also thanks to the media empire that his business acolytes had managed to build in the meantime. The landslide victory was followed, in 2011, by hasty amendments of the constitution and a series of laws, and by swift changes in various government-controlled boards, councils etc., thus consolidating power across public institutions. Orbán embarked on a campaign to rein in various institutions outside the narrow frame of government – 'on a Gramscian programme of social transformation',[141] following

---

139. Ibid., p. 48.
140. Ibid., p. 57.
141. Rachman, p. 97.

the school of thought of the Italian Marxist Gramsci who saw power residing in cultural institutions. Indeed, as we shall see, this has not been a simple battle for power and money only, but also for the souls of Hungarians – the so-called culture wars. The previous dominance of the political left was thus replaced by an equally complete domination of the Orbán-led right. According to Lendvai, it was all about mere will to power, only superficially hidden under a care for traditional values, undoubtedly important to a large part of the Hungarian electorate. Apart from the appeal of referring to Christian values, the trauma of Trianon (the loss of territory after World War I according to the Treaty of Trianon) played a key part in gaining such strong support:[142] 'No Hungarian reacts with indifference when it comes to the architectural gems and memorials, the graves of mighty kings and the birth houses of great poets, in the old Hungarian towns in Transylvania (Romania), 'Upper Hungary' (Slovakia) and Vojvodina (Serbia),' writes Lendvai.[143] Orbán has continued to play on 'two predominant elements of Hungarian self-image – the victim myth and the will to survive'.[144]

This complete domination of Fidesz loyalists eventually opened the door to widespread corruption, which Lendvai argues can no longer be compared to the corruption of left-wing governments in the 2002-2010 period (to which the author is by no means lenient). It also led to controversial relations between Hungary on the one hand, and China and Russia on the other, as also evident again years later during the Russian aggression in Ukraine. Orbán's conquest of Hungary continued with his re-election in 2014, in 2018 and

142. Lendvai, p. 38.
143. Lendvai, p. 88.
144. Lendvai, p. 194.

again in 2022, and during this time he became a Europe-wide voice of social conservatism amd the European right, for example, through his contacts with Marine Le Pen. Given the commendation by Steve Bannon, Orbán positioned himself as a social conservative even on the global scale. 'The experience of gaining a global audience and lecturing affluent Western Europeans about the future of politics was intoxicating for the Hungarian leader. For decades, ever since the fall of the Berlin Wall, the post-Soviet countries had been cast in the role of students and supplicants. [...] Now it was their turn.'[145] Or as Orbán proclaimed: 'We used to think that Europe was our future. Today we know that we are the future of Europe.'[146] This was no longer copying of the West; something original was coming from Central Europe, something declared as truly European – Central Europe was at the centre of attention indeed. 'In a spiritual sense, the West has moved to Central Europe,' said Orbán in a speech in July 2022. 'The two halves of Europe are locked in a battle... The West has rejected Central Europe's desire to allow each nation to live as they like, and they continue to fight Central Europe to change us to be like them,' he added.[147] (As a result of racist undertones in the same speech, a close collaborator of Orbán decided to resign.) Orbán's position on the global conservative scene was again confirmed in his prominent appearance at the annual Conservative Political Action Conference (CPAC) in the United States in August 2022.[148]

145. Rachman, p. 93.

146. As cited in Rachman, p. 93.

147. dailynewshungary.com https://dailynewshungary.com/orban-hungarians-are-not-a-mixed-race-and-does-not-want-to-become-one/ (Retrieved 25 July 2022).

148. https://www.washingtonpost.com/nation/2022/08/04/viktor-orban-cpac-dallas-speech/

One may label Mr Orbán a populist (or worse), but to any populist, real (and not just alleged, as it was the case during the Communist times) support is essential. And that support in Hungary (as in Poland) appears to be real, not enforced or only bought with perks. Only to condemn it, does little good; one has to understand the drivers for such trends. The 'threat' of migrants, the urban-rural divide, the nostalgia for a far greater pre-Trianon Hungary (and lack of reflection on the feelings of non-Hungarian peoples ruled by Hungarians, sometimes in brutal fashion, as was the case during World War II in Hungarian-occupied zones), and the preference for traditional values have been already mentioned. Lendvai adds that liberal and left-wing parties were also not able to present a clear and credible political agenda,[149] something that, as we shall see, also played a role in Poland.

In upholding these arguments, Orbán and his party often invoked their alleged ideological arch-enemy, Mr Soros, even to the point of recourse to antisemitism, further adding to the parallels to pre-World War II Europe and the advent of Fascism at the time. Soros' support to various NGOs, promoting liberal values and the cause of migrants often, though not initially (at one point even a young Mr Orbán was the recipient), run contrary to the socially conservative policies of Mr Orbán and his ilk. What was certainly not helpful to Soros was his background in speculative finance operations. Even Soros himself 'expressed doubts about the social and economic impact of the globalised financial markets, in which he made his fortune.'[150] And Emily Tamkin, the author of *The Influence of Soros*, admits that there has been a 'tension between Soros' financial abilities and his

---

149. Lendvai, p. 131
150. Rachman, p. 207.

philanthropic ambitions'[151] and concludes that in that respect 'Soros is at best paradoxical and at worst hypocritical'.[152] To what extent his grand and commendable philanthropic work is compromised thus remains to be analysed. But what is more important is to ask whether the liberal agenda, as pursued by Soros and the NGOs financed by him, is in its entirety and as a whole something that best represents the agreed set of European values, something that must be upheld at all costs. And, at the same time, is social conservatism, as seen in Eastern Europe, already a definite departure from Western liberalism? In what areas or in what way? Was it really unavoidable – on both sides – to arrive at a situation in which Soros' efforts are met with such strong opposition, precisely there, where they are most needed? At the same time, conservatives in Central Europe should ask themselves whether Mr Orbán and Mr Kaczyński are also the best placed and most legitimate representatives of the views of Central and Eastern Europe, even of its conservative cohort. Also, could – and under what circumstances – Muslim migrants in the 2015/2016 crisis have received a better welcome by Eastern Europe, as they should, given the region's professed Christian values?

These are questions which are – notwithstanding Orbán's clever utilisation of his compatriots' hearts and minds – rarely being asked and even more rarely answered. It is much easier to simply reject the opposition to Soros' agenda as an unacceptably conservative social engineering or a right-wing extremism; even Fascism is a word used here and there. But neo-Marxists, post-modern neo-liberals, Putin in the case of Ukraine and Stalin at the time of his invasion of Poland used

151. Tamkin, E, *The Influence of Soros*, HarperCollins, 2020, p.66.
152. Ibid., p. 182.

Fascist-labelling to justify their actions too. Fascism 'suffered from an excess of definition. To cry "fascist!" suggested a lazy equation with Adolf Hitler, total war and the Holocaust. The far left further devalued the term by hurling it around to denounce everyone from capitalist bosses to mildly disciplinarian schoolteachers,' adds Timothy Garton Ash.[153]

Similar accusations have been made against the other *enfant terrible* of the region – Poland. In 2020, Andrzej Duda, a representative of the conservative Law and Justice party, won a second term as President of Poland, consolidating the grip on power of the Law and Justice Party of Mr Kaczyński. His victory confirmed that the main Polish political divide does not lie between the left and the right, not even between the true democrats and post-communists, but mainly between the socially conservative and traditionally Catholic countryside and liberal urban Poland, although – and this is significant and interesting – the Law and Justice party has been opposed not only by the Post-Communists (SLD) and the Liberals (a coalition gathered around the Conservative-Liberal Civic Platform), but also by a coalition around the central, Christian Democratic Polish People's Party. Furthermore, and to make things even more complicated, President Duda is considered a moderate among the Law and Justice loyalists, who in turn have far more radical coalition partners further down on the right. To complete the picture of the Polish party political landscape, a potentially promising alternative to Law and Justice is emerging in the moderately conservative *Poland 2050* party of which we may hear more in the future.

---

153. 'For a fascist revival look to Moscow, not Rome', *Financial Times*, 30 September 2022.

In *Poland's Constitutional Breakdown*, Polish constitutional lawyer Wojciech Sadurski describes in detail and convincingly what actually happened in Poland when the Law and Justice party took power for the second time in 2015. The party had already led the government between 2005 and 2007, in a coalition with other parties, but a more definite policy pattern, the one we know now, started to emerge only after 2015. It all began with the controversial replacement of constitutional judges whose terms expired in 2015, with Sadurski acknowledging that the then outgoing liberal government of the Civic Platform had already made some of the same mistakes.[154] However, with a two-thirds majority in parliament, the new government gained such a majority in the Constitutional Court that it was 'safe' from possible proceedings before it.

In the second step, the government amended the legislation governing the elections to the Judicial Council, thus gaining a strong majority in it as well. It then did the same with the Supreme Court and with the reorganisation of the lower courts. Then, in 2016, the government merged the roles of public prosecutor and Minister of Justice. All this happened without the government changing the constitution, as was done in Hungary by Orbán, but rather by simply using the overwhelming majority in the parliament and consequently in the Constitutional Court.[155] Technically speaking then, the letter of the law has been followed – but so was the case in many authoritarian and even totalitarian systems in history, the critics were saying.

The parliamentary super-majority of the Law and Justice party was the principal vehicle through which the entire law-

154. Sadurski, W, *Poland's Constitutional Breakdown*, Oxford University Press 2019, p. 62.
155. Sadurski, p. 84.

making process was carried out with lightning speed. The government also intervened in the legislation governing the recruitment of civil servants,[156] thus allowing for political appointments there too. So-called Polonisation of the media followed: about 200 journalists on public TV were fired[157] and replaced by right-wing journalists. The government also launched an initiative to re-Polonise private media with the aim of snatching them from foreign hands, especially from German media companies. Amendments to the legislation governing demonstrations were also adopted that made such gatherings more difficult to organise.[158]

In response to all these moves by the Polish government, the European Commission in December 2017 initiated the so-called Article 7 procedure. (It was triggered for Hungary in September 2018.) Article 7 of the Treaty on the European Union envisages a possibility of suspension of certain rights of a member state, if found by four fifths of the Council to be at 'clear risk of serious breach' of the fundamental values of the EU. However, to date, the Council has never gone that far.

Interestingly, Sadurski does not see any special ideology behind the actions by the Polish government, not even a Catholic one. He believes that Jaroslaw Kaczyński – the grey eminence of current Polish political establishment, although a very religious man, who likes to play the card of Catholicism – will eventually get rid of the influence of the Church too. His ideology is said to be based on his conspiratory interpretation of the tragic plane crash in Russia's Smolensk (on an official trip to Russia) in 2010, which killed the entire Polish state top echelon led by the president, Jaroslaw's brother Lech

---

156. Sadurski, p. 136.
157. Sadurski, p. 138.
158. Sadurski, p. 151.

Kaczyński. Putin and Polish liberals are believed to be somehow involved, according to this conspiracy narrative.

In any event, the accident strengthened Jarosław Kaczyński's belief that the world is (still) a hostile place and that the country's leadership will be taken over by self-proclaimed independent ombudsmen, judicial organs and non-governmental organisations, as well as Putin's Russia. (In his attitude to the latter, he is very different from Orbán.)

According to Sadurski, the ideological motivation of the Law and Justice party is not so much about confronting the remnants of the communist elite in Poland (most of it has been removed through the process of lustration anyway), but mainly about the fear of the traditionally thinking countryside of things liberal, global, multicultural, etc., something argued by Krastev too. In other words, Law and Justice's repeated victory is supposed to be the result of the mindset of rural Poland that has also not benefitted equally from the introduction of a market economy and democracy, despite Poland's favourable macroeconomic position under the previous liberal government. As far as the rural-urban divide goes, this sounds very much like Hungary.

Sadurski admits that before its 2015 defeat, the liberal Civic Platform collapsed, tainted with corruption scandals, having lost contact with voters, especially in rural areas. After the election victory, Law and Justice not only, as explained earlier, problematically interfered in the judiciary and overcame political opponents wherever it could, but also took good care to institute a generous social policy (including an often cited universal child allowance), which many Polish families find essential to make ends meet. All this was possible due to the favourable macroeconomic position of Poland that continued during Law and Justice's term of office, including the rather liberal economic policies of the otherwise conservative Jarosław Kaczyński.

The author sees in all this a typical populist approach, a 'delegative democracy'[159] or a 'plebiscitary autocracy',[160] although he does not deny that Kaczyński enjoys a broad public support, which he is able, like Mr Orbán, to skilfully garner and master. He stresses that the voters of Law and Justice 'have a sense of distance from the cultural values of the liberal elite, and in particular they feel anxiety related to immigration and multiculturalism, and this sense is not clearly correlated with their relative socio-economic deprivation.'[161] So it is not all about the economy and the lesser standing of the rural areas. And, one may add, instead of Trianon in the Hungarian case, there is here the 2010 Smolensk tragedy, that resembles in many ways another tragic Polish experience with the Soviet Union, that of the 1940 Katyn Forest massacre. In fact, the Polish delegation was on its way to a memorial event at the site of this massacre, in which nearly 22,000 Polish military elite and intellectuals were executed by the Soviets.

But Sadurski's notion that 'Polish democratic backsliding does not have an ideological blueprint'[162] is perhaps missing the point. He himself identifies sources of Polish populism: a generally good level of delivery on election promises by the government, above all on welfare benefits, effective propaganda in the media, appeal to negative emotions, political polarisation, and weakened institutions.[163] He cited analysts, otherwise critical of the Law and Justice party,

---

159. Sadurski, p. 242.
160. Sadurski, p. 248.
161. Sadurski, p. 169.
162. Sadurski, p. 249.
163. Sadurski, pp. 175 – 179.

who describe the perception of the liberal establishment by the Law and Justice party's voters: 'The incumbent elite are seen not only as arrogant and corrupt, but at the same time so cosmopolitan and anti-national that they are willing, for whatever reasons (to allay their own sense of guilt?) to let in masses of migrants and thus dilute the sense of nation-based unity and community.'[164] Clearly, this is not just about due democratic process and not even just about the economy, but about substance – or ideology, if you will.

Sadurski eventually adds that 'explaining how xenophobia, anti-establishmentarism, and illiberalism could have come together in a single package [...] is key to a compelling story about the sources of Kaczyński's seduction of a significant segment of Polish electorate.'[165] (One could add that such explanation would be helpful also to explain other cases of populism.) But he stops here, as do many critics of the situation in Poland under the government of Law and Justice. So too does Anne Applebaum in her *Twilight of Democracy*,[166] where she describes with some pain the growing polarisation of Polish society, affecting also her personal relationships with many (former) Polish friends. But she is unable to offer an explanation of the root causes of this polarisation. She seems not to go beyond criticism of the populism of the Law and Justice party, though she does acknowledge that in Poland and other former Communist countries there is a 'widespread feeling that the rules of competition are flawed because the reforms of the 1990s – when mass privatisation and the imposition of free-market rules transformed the economies – allowed too

---

164. Sadurski, p. 172.

165. Sadurski, p. 173.

166. Applebaum, A, *Twilight of Democracy: The Seductive Lure of Authoritarianism*, Doubleday, 2020.

many former Communists to recycle their political power.' (I have described this painful process in the previous chapter.) Yet she also believes that this argument of the negative role of recycled former Communists 'which felt so important a quarter century ago, seems thin and superficial now.'[167] She thinks that populist politicians in Poland and Hungary are using 'restorative nostalgics' and are, above all, 'mythmakers and architects, builders of monuments and founders of nationalist political projects.'[168]

Poland and Hungary are the usual examples given of illiberal (Central) Europe. Other countries of the region seem to fare better – or perhaps it only seems so. Slovakia, despite the infamous case of the murder of an investigative journalist Ján Kuciak in 2018, is now better known for its liberal President Mrs Čaputová. (In the Netherlands too, an investigative journalist, Petr R. de Vries, was killed in Amsterdam in 2021, though it is true that no political connection to the murder was suggested. That was not the case with the murder of Maltese journalist Daphne Caruana Galizia in 2017. A sign of parallels and similarities between Eastern and Southern Europe?) Still, there are issues with the judiciary in Slovakia.[169] Baltic countries seem not to be particularly moved by populists: the agenda there is overwhelmed by the Russian threat, which continues to provide a shared base for national consensus. Still, the Estonian EKRE party received some prominence for its Eurosceptic and anti-elite stance.[170]

---

167. Ibid., p. 28.
168. Ibid., p. 74.
169. See e.g. https://www.cambridge.org/core/journals/german-law-journal/article/capturing-the-judiciary-from-inside-the-story-of-judicial-selfgovernance-in-slovakia/C6D69845D7192FB732181E97F93C6B2A
170. Naylor, p. 146.

The case of the Czech Republic, the country in the region with the longest democratic tradition, is interesting. There, successive governments of (non-Communist) Social Democrats or liberal conservatives remained broadly aligned with the liberal democratic consensus, all the more so after the Russian aggression against Ukraine. Yet Mr Andrej Babiš, an ultra-rich businessman who appealed to very diverse groups of voters and was seen as a populist by many, twice served as Prime Minister and runs for President in 2023. By the same token, Miloš Zeman, the country's incumbent president, was up until the Russian invasion of Ukraine known for his pro-Russian and anti-immigrants stance.

In Croatia, power is often seen as being passed back and forth between a form of post-Communists and conservatives, both with strong patriotic undertones. In Slovenia, three consecutive elections (2014, 2018 and 2022) have propelled to the position of Prime Minister almost complete novices in politics, with their respective political parties established only a couple of months before elections. There, as seen by Slovenian conservative voters, a practically uncontested and near-complete dominance of politics, business, media and civil society originates in various leftist parties and groups, and has only briefly been interrupted by right-wing leader Janez Janša, often cited for his flirting with Orbán, though he lacked his Hungarian counterpart's majority in the parliament. It was during these short periods of Janša's government that leftist opposition and many NGOs were most vocal about alleged breaches of the rule of law and pressure exerted over the media. At the same time, Mr Janša was also accused of being a Fascist, while simultaneously receiving death threats, both public and in private, which he claimed were not all duly followed up by prosecutors.

Romania and Bulgaria also have their problems with the rule

of law, holding them up for years before the gates of Schengen. As late as mid-2022, Politico bluntly put it: 'Bulgaria has been struggling to liberate itself from the influence of a web of oligarch *mafiosi* with deep ties in the parliament and judiciary.'[171]

Such bluntness, used by reporters and politicians alike, is sometimes selective and ignores problems that liberal democracies face in Western Europe too. To say the least, fragmentation and the abandoning of classic mainstream parties have been a phenomenon across Europe, not only in Central Europe. 'Support for democracy has plummeted across the Western world since the fall of the Berlin Wall.'[172] The positive impact of the return of democracy to Europe's East has had only a transitory character – both in the East and the West. The latter is now preoccupied with waves of crisis – terrorism, financial crisis, migration crisis, Brexit, Ukraine, energy crisis. In the east, in Central Europe, the danger for young democracies and populism comes not only (or not as much) from the sources just mentioned, but also from those that are largely unknown to the West. These origins are complex, write Stephen Holmes and Ivan Krastev, 'but they partly lie in the humiliation associated with the uphill struggle to become, at best, an inferior copy of a superior model'.[173] Their analysis of the worldwide populism sees Russians 'cynically simulating the Western democracy', the Chinese 'voraciously borrowing Western technology' and Central Europeans doing nothing of these.[174]

171. https://www.politico.eu/newsletter/brussels-playbook/kaliningrad-simmers-enlargement-hypocrisies-renew-and-bulgaria/ (retrieved on 23.6.2022).
172. Luce, E, *The Retreat of Western Liberalism*, Little, Brown, 2017, p. 121.
173. Krastev, I, Holmes, S, *The Light that Failed*, Allen Lane, 2019, p. 22.
174. Krastev, I, Holmes, S, p. 25.

One other origin of Eastern European populism in their view is a 'delayed backlash against several decades of identity-denial politics, otherwise known as Westernisation, which began in 1989'.[175] In that respect they are critical of the fact that the West has forgotten that 'liberalism, too, works best within the context of politically bounded communities'.[176]

Indeed, a number of Western European countries have seen their national cohesion tested in recent years, from the UK in the case of Scottish aspirations to independence to Spain in the case of Catalonia. And in the US, polarisation of society has reached such an extent that – particularly following the 6 January riots – there was talk about the possibility of a civil war.

As in the West, meritocracy, as one of the essential foundations of Western civilisation, began to show its drawbacks in the East too, even if it manifested itself differently. Here, 'meritocracy is additionally offensive in the region's historical context because of the privileged access to economic success provided, after 1989, to those who occupied important political positions in the previous oppressive system. What distinguished 1989 from all previous revolutions was the ease with which the ostensibly "dethroned" elites managed to preserve their power and influence.'[177] This is the legacy of the old-boys network, of former regime apparatchiks. While (in Poland and Hungary) this may indeed serve as an excuse for a simple power-grab, it is – in the eyes of conservative voters – a real problem in Slovenia, where the former elite managed to maintain a fair degree of legitimacy by opting for the country's independence and by showing the will to transform, at least on the surface, early on in the transition process. Their dominance

---

175. Ibid., p. 57.
176. Ibid., p. 58.
177. Ibid., p. 67.

appears to be so overwhelming that it largely goes unnoticed by those on the same side of the divide. As one of the leading left-wing national TV commentators Marcel Štefančič said in a rare moment of acknowledgement, at the height of the campaign against right-wing Prime Minister Janša's attempts to have a more balanced national TV broadcaster by promoting journalists closer to Mr Janša: 'There are fuc**** more of us than them. They are only a few and we know exactly who they are.'[178] Soon after that, Janša was voted out of office in a landslide victory by a political novice Robert Golob who became Prime Minister in June 2022 and announced his intention to depoliticise the media and public administration, with expert competence as the only criteria for staffing. But expertise in a post-Communist context is often a code word for experts of a certain political affiliation, while the political persuasion of other civil servants is publicly exposed and frowned upon, as noted by the critics.[179]

The same goes for the judiciary, which was at the centre of attention for Kaczyński and also Orbán, and earned Poland numerous reprimands by the European Commission and also cases in the Court of the EU. The Article 7 case was triggered against both countries. A special Rule of Law mechanism was also designed at the Council of the EU level to monitor the Rule of Law situation in all EU countries, but Poland and Hungary have been its main targets. Within this mechanism, Slovenia

---

178. https://topnews.si/2022/05/03/video-novinarje-te-slavne-mogocne-hise-pozivam-ce-boste-kak-del-moje-danasnje-izjave-uvrstili-v-svoj-prispevek-pa-vam-bodo-rekli-da-ga-izrezite-se-uprite-recite-ne-marcel-stefancic-na-prote/ (translated from Slovenian, retrieved on 15.6.2022).

179. Two of the chief critics of Janša's media policy among the journalists were then made government spokesperson and spokesperson for the new Prime Minister's party, respectively.

during the two-year mandate of Prime Minister Janša also received some unwanted attention and criticism. However, the European Commission's Rule of Law reports appear to have failed to account for a deep-seated belief across the centre-right electorate in Slovenia (and elsewhere) that the judiciary is far from the ideal of an independent and unbiased institution. This part of the electorate believes, rightly or wrongly, that the judiciary is stuffed not with Janša's loyalists, but with left-wingers, affiliated with the network of old-boys from the Communist past. The capture of state institutions is here believed to have been made by left-wing populists and conspirators, not by right-wing populists and social conservatives. Such a view may be wrong or exaggerated, but the problem is that it does not receive proper attention by the drafters of the Commission's reports whatsoever. Could it then, after all, be that some of Law and Justice's accusations against the Polish judiciary have indeed been correct? Sadurski dismisses this notion and traces the legislative actions by Law and Justice governments to their populist, anti-establishment character. But still, could it be that institutions of the system in post-Communist countries, and their resistance to change, have indeed been marked by the remnants of the Communist past? This possibility was also discarded almost immediately by the European Commission and Western Governments, the latter only having an experience of anti-establishment forces coming from the radical right (and to a lesser extent the radical left). Current Polish and Hungarian governments (and the short-lived governments of Janez Janša in Slovenia) proved incapable of presenting a better argument for that case, or perhaps lacked legitimacy for that. In Slovenia, the 2020-2022 cabinet of Mr Janša tried in vain to point out the shortcomings of the methodology used by the European Commission in drafting the Rule of Law reports, based almost exclusively on media reports and interviews with the NGOs, most of which were overwhelmingly and openly hostile to Janša's government.

After a long political and legal wrangling at the EU level, in 2022 Poland finally gave up, at least partially, and promised to roll back some of the most controversial steps (e.g. the establishment of a disciplinary chamber for judges) in order to avail itself of EU post-pandemic recovery funds. Something similar was being arranged in Hungary at the time of writing of this book. At the centre of Brussels' demands are procurement transparency in the Hungarian case and reversal of reforms that were seen as political disciplining of judges in the case of Poland.[180]

The principle of the Rule of Law has indeed became a key concern and the central theme of EU debate when it comes to Poland and Hungary and the rest of Central Europe. There seem to be real problems in those two countries: 'Instead of enriching Western liberal constitutional values with their post-communist experience, these states have rather started a new populist movement in the form of constitutional backsliding whose final objective is the creation of an illiberal state.'[181] The two authors of this statement are also critical of the European Commission and Western EU countries for ignoring for too long the 'constitutional backsliding', especially of Orbán's 'constitutional capture of the state' and of the 'democratic crisis' in Poland. Entering the EU was hardly enough: 'The

---

180. 'Hungary pledges more rule-of-law concessions to avoid EU funding cuts', *Financial Times*, 26 September 2022, and 'Poland takes steps towards unlocking EU recovery funds', *Financial Times*, 11 October 2022.
181. Avbelj, M, Letnar Černič, J, Justinek, G, *The Impact of European Institutions on the Rule of Law and Democracy: Slovenia and Beyond*, Hart Publishing, 2020, p. 3.

biggest progress, indeed a breakthrough, under the influence of EU law was thus engendered at the pre-accession stage. Later on, with the celebratory mood setting in, pervaded by a growing complacency of being the best pupil in the class, these formal legal benchmarks started losing their influence. The discrepancy between formal requirements and actual practice started to grow, but EU membership has continued to force the stakeholders in Slovenia to stick to their practice of organised hypocrisy.'[182]

Like Sadurski, Avbelj and Letnar Černič offer a devastating criticism of illiberal democracy in Poland (and Hungary), but they also point to the lesser known – and quite specific – case of Slovenia. As said earlier, the two are critical of European politicians and academics for 'a notable lack of in-depth research focusing on democracy and the rule of law in Central and Eastern Europe'[183] though 'the elusiveness of the meaning, or rather meanings, of the rule of law in theory has also hindered its operationalisation in practice' because of the 'open ended character of the rule of law'.[184] They find this absence of a detailed study of the quality of democracy in Central and Eastern Europe quite disturbing 'for this crisis is truly a systematic one and runs deep in the very mindset and comprehensive modus operandi of the post-communist societies in CEE [Central and Eastern European] countries'.[185] But the most important and quite unique contribution the two authors make to the debate on the democratic backlash in Eastern Europe is to follow. Not only in Poland and Hungary, but also in the rest of the region the rule of law 'appears to

---

182. Ibid., p. 238.
183. Ibid., p. 10.
184. Ibid., p. 5.
185. Ibid., p. 7.

have been, since the fall of the Iron Curtain, under attack from *nouveau riche* elites very much connected to the former totalitarian regimes. Old practices of corruption, nepotism, clientelism and "dirty togetherness" have not only not been eradicated, but remain present in the centre of institutional and public space in certain CEE countries. Most of those countries have not undertaken a fully-fledged reform of the rule of law and have retained a post-socialist formal and authoritarian mentality'.[186]

For Avbelj and Letnar Černič, it is about 'fundamental misunderstandings by old member states and EU institutions about the sociopolitical nature of these countries. [...] [i]n many ways the outcome of a deliberate, even if benign, neglect of the real sociopolitical state of affairs in these countries by the old member states and Brussels-based institutions out of a desire to make the EU big bang enlargement of 2004 a success story', in which 'to a certain extent the international and supranational political as well as economic alliances played their role too. When these alliances have been undermined or even broken – largely under the duress of the financial and economic crisis that began in 2008 – the Potemkin village of CEE states irreversibly started collapsing too'.[187]

According to the authors, Slovenia is a good example of such a Potemkin village. There, with the exceptions of short spells of government by the centre-right Prime Minister Janez Janša, the country has been for most of the 30 years of independence run by coalitions dominated by various leftist parties and 'the capture of the state by the post-communist left and their economic allies has gone uncriticised, unsanctioned

---

186. Ibid., p. 7.
187. Ibid., p. 9.

and has been taken as part of the new normal of the slightly peculiar Slovenian capitalist model'.[188] Furthermore, 'the former communist elites have almost completely usurped the public institutions where they have advanced their own arbitrary interests,'[189] so that 'Slovenia's model of de facto political and economic continuity with the pre-democratic system has permitted its elites to hold on to control of the country without any openly authoritarian tendencies, capture of the state or constitutional backsliding.'[190]

This quite unique 'leftist Orbánisation' has thus gone largely unnoticed. Essential in this was the role of the media, as it was the 'elite's economic and political control over the media', which 'proved decisive. For it was exactly the media with a strong left-centre bias which facilitated, justified and defended the conquering of the Slovenian public and private sphere by the leftist post-socialist elite.'[191] Contrary to what is normally expected of the media in a liberal democracy 'the impact of the press on the functioning of Slovenia's constitutional democracy and the rule of law has been in the prevailing sense weak or even negative. The Slovenian media has been, with few exceptions, one of the actors most responsible for the deficient workings of the country's constitutional democracy as it has at different levels directly and indirectly affected electoral process, thereby interfering with the proper functioning of all the three primary branches of government. Even more conspicuous has been the role of RTV Slovenia [public radio and TV broadcaster], which has in recent decades failed to provide independent and pluralist

---

188. Ibid., p. 240.
189. Ibid., p. 51.
190. Ibid., p. 31.
191. Ibid., p. 30.

news reporting.'[192] Given the role that the media are supposed to have in a well-functioning liberal democracy, such criticism is indeed devastating.

The authors try to look for the root causes of this rarely heard version of what happened in what in so many respects has been the model among the Central European countries. Among them are 'systematic and widespread human rights violations (1945-90)', i.e. during the communist period and as described in the first part of this book. Furthermore, after the changes the 'Constitutional Court has [...] contributed to the formation of the formal standards of the rule of law and human rights', however, 'its impact on the reform of the mentality of civil servants, public employees and holders of public offices and the daily appreciation of the rule of law in practice has so far been limited [...] Slovenia, as most CEE countries, therefore appears to suffer from the fact that liberal democratic values have not been fully internalised due to resistance from institutional elites and ordinary people'. For this reason, 'it has been very difficult to move from the rule of law de jure to the rule of law de facto in the life of democratic institutions of transitional states'.[193]

The two Slovenian academics are particularly concerned with the judiciary (in Slovenia), finding that 'the overall institutional set-up, modus operandi, material conditions and, finally, the mindset of the people working in the Slovenian judiciary are, ultimately, not conducive to the kind of system of justice required by the rule of law in so-called well-ordered states'.[194]

Continuing looking at the roots of the state of the rule of law in Central Europe, the authors also warn about 'socioeconomic

---

192. Ibid., p. 173.
193. Ibid., pp. 34 – 54.
194. Ibid., p. 121.

populism' which 'defends the values and the interests of the unprivileged class'.[195] Lack of economic pluralism in Slovenia is exposed, whereby 'control over and the occupancy of the formal institutions are much less important since power lurks in the economic monopoly of the state and private companies attached to it'.[196] For this reason 'in the more "progressive" Slovenia, where formal institutions have long been in the service of informal interests closely connected to the state-run economy, there is simply no need for authoritarian pushes' as we know them from Hungary and Poland.[197] In other words, the authors believe that the capture of the state (and civil society) by the same interest network is of such an extent and runs so deep that controversial actions by those in formal power – that would otherwise raise eyebrows in Brussels – are not even needed. To the contrary: it is precisely the attempts (no doubt some controversial too) to alter the situation described that appear and are presented as contrary to the rule of law, freedom of expressions and the system of checks and balances. This seemed to be evident during Janša's 2020-2022 government, when – admittedly often clumsy and sometimes controversial – attempts to pluralise publicly funded media were met with orchestrated large-scale protests and impassioned appeals to the European Commission and domestic and international press freedom watchdogs. Occasionally violent, these protests against the centre-right government of Mr Janša during the Covid crisis, mainly targeting the health-related prevention measures, were completely free of any nationalist tone, though certainly not of resentment and often also hatred, even instilling some fear among the conservative population.

195. Ibid., p. 243.
196. Ibid., p. 246.
197. Ibid., p. 246.

Such was the extent of this opposition that it led to a landslide election victory of a previously little known opponent, who had announced a complete revision of the entire legislation and personnel appointments done during the two years of Mr Janša's government. The very legitimacy of that government was put under question and its policies labelled not only as populist, but often also as Fascist.

To summarise, the far greater impact of populism in Central Europe (compared to Western Europe) 'can thus be generally explained with the help of three constitutive variables of a constitutional democracy: institutionalisation; civic awareness and active citizenship; and finally economic pluralism'. Due to a historically shorter and/or weaker record in all these three areas, Central and Eastern Europe was hit harder when it comes to 'destabilisation of constitutional democracy'. This explains why 'Western European countries, even when some of them, such as Greece, Portugal and even Ireland, suffered severely from the global financial crisis, have not upended their constitutional democracies to the same extent as has been happening in Hungary or Poland',[198] or, as Avbelj and Letnar Černič suggest in Slovenia, where wide popular support is claimed by leftist political forces.

The two Slovenian authors are also repeatedly critical of foreign observers, even international NGOs: 'Overall, one can discern heterogeneity in the pronouncements of the various regional and international human rights bodies as to human rights crises in Slovenia. The majority of these bodies have too often only pinpointed recurring themes always highlighted by ministries and publicly funded NGOs. For those reasons, some of them have turned a blind eye to

---

198. Ibid., p. 245.

practices affecting fundamental human rights issues such as the right to fair, independent and impartial trial, protection of human dignity against the abuses of state authorities, and the lack of transitional justice measures. [...] This unequal approach has contributed to the creation of a public image that only certain human rights issues are of concern in Slovenia. [...] Such a selective approach has certainly been politically biased, unequal and inefficient.'[199] In other words, attention to the shortcomings in the area of the rule of law can be – and sometimes apparently is – also partisan and biased. As we know from the infamous stories of the Central European University in Budapest and Soros-affiliated NGOs, Orbán pushed the issue of NGOs to the limits and exploited it for his attack on Soros and the opposition. But is it possible after all, and politically correct, to ask a question about the legitimacy and accountability of NGOs? Or is it that the NGOs and media are the modern priesthood that cannot be challenged? Who or what provides checks and balances for them? These are the kinds of questions that may indeed sound heretical in long-established democracies, where independent media and NGOs have emerged as a result of centuries-long process. But can that be equally said of media and NGOs in former Communist countries? These issues remain unexplored by the critics of the state of the rule of law in post-Communist countries, while Mr Orbán, with his handling of the Central European University in Budapest, certainly does not provide a helpful answer either.

However, notwithstanding their criticism of the rather superficial approach to the study of the state of the rule of law in Eastern Europe, Avbelj and Letnar Černič warn against politicians and, even more, academics justifying the truly

---

199. Ibid., p. 85.

troubling trends in Central Europe by describing the situation in these countries as having 'simply developed their own version of constitutionalism'. They find that unacceptable from the point of view of European values, that must indeed remain one and the same, valid for the whole Union. Instead, to rectify such a situation (both in Central and the rest of Europe), the authors call for measures at the EU level, such as deepening of the monetary union with the banking, fiscal, and social union. Another important area to make European countries' constitutional democracies more resilient has, according to the authors, to do with security, including border security. These steps should be complemented by structural reforms of the EU. However, when it comes to 'removing "dirty togetherness" from the institutional life', they admit that – in addition to reforms that they propose for executive and legislative branches of national governments, the constitutional framework, the judiciary, media and the private sector – 'how to proceed further is more difficult to answer. The most straightforward answers are to reform the mentality and bet on the education of a younger generation.'[200]

But educated minds, internalised values, meritocracy, transparency, integrity, professionalism of civil service etc. do not exist in a vacuum; they are attributes of holders of offices that these people have to internalise. The book stops short of explaining how to achieve that in practice, how to deal with informal old networks or how to roll back controversial legislative measures taken by governments – these would in many instances require a super-majority in respective parliaments that more liberal governments in the future may not be able to attain. It also does not touch upon the issue

---

200. Ibid., pp. 246, 250.

of a need to strengthen the legitimacy and accountability of increasingly powerful NGOs.

Finally, the authors do not address the issue of the very real support that populist leaders, right and left, enjoy among the voters. How can one change the mentality of the voters? The usual reply would be through education and media, but these again seem to be compromised in many of the post-Communist societies. And what should the EU do, now that these countries are firmly in the EU? While legal procedures (referral of a Member State to the Court of the EU by the European Commission), political steps (like the Article 7 discussion) and peer reviews (Rule of Law dialogue within the Council) could be helpful in some instances, castigation and bashing will not help; rather, it will further alienate some of what are still the most EU-enthusiastic member states, at a time the EU needs cohesion and outer strength. Tony Barber, FT commentator and harsh critic of the current Polish and Hungarian governments, concedes: 'The EU is guilty of double standards insofar as other countries with deficiencies in the rule of law, including in Western Europe, have never come under the same pressure from Brussels as Hungary and Poland. True, the abuses are more serious in Budapest and Warsaw. But other governments in Central and Eastern Europe dislike what they see as the EU's older member states lecturing the newer ones as if they are children in a classroom. Most were deprived of national freedom in the Soviet era and are more sensitive on matters of sovereignty than many Western Europeans grasp.'[201]

So what is to be done? At the very minimum, the EU should start to be honest about specific problems that exist in

201. Barber, T, 'The EU must be tougher with Poland on the rule of law', *Financial Times*, 2 August 2021.

post-communist member states, and analyse the state of the
Rule of Law much more in detail, taking into consideration
also historical obstacles to the full implementation of the
essential principles of liberal democracy. This is what many
on the centre-right expected when more than ten years ago the
Netherlands floated the idea of a rule of law review within the
EU, although this was linked to the Dutch opposition to the
entry of Bulgaria and Romania into Schengen. In April 2013 the
Dutch idea was presented at the Council in Brussels, though it
did not initially receive an enthusiastic welcome and the press
release only read that 'the Council took note of an initiative
by Denmark, Finland, Germany and the Netherlands for a
new and more effective mechanism to safeguard fundamental
values in member states and had a first comprehensive
discussion on the subject'.[202] At the time, I reported myself
from The Hague about this idea with vigour, in a belief that
such mechanism could help various European countries to
deal with their different historical legacies. But by the time the
idea developed into a quite influential mechanism, any hopes
for a more sensitive, finely tuned instrument evaporated.

After all, similar totalitarian legacies, acting as potential
obstacles to democratic development, may exist in other
European countries that in the twentieth century experienced
a totalitarian or authoritarian rule, although this is rarely
talked about. We know of considerable post-World War II
denazification efforts in Germany. Less zealous were political
stakeholders in post-war Austria and Italy, where remnants of
the past have in some quarters remained evident, for example,
in the less than exemplary treatment of the Slovenian minority.
(In Italy, even a rather benign turn to the right in Rome might

---

202. https://ec.europa.eu/commission/presscorner/detail/en/PRES_13_153

in Trieste/Trst region translate into unfriendly minority policies. This is much more the case when such right parties are flirting with the Fascist legacy – something we should bear in mind at the moment.) Spanish transition and reconciliation was relatively widely publicised and could provide some useful advice to Central and Eastern Europe, as could perhaps that in Greece and Portugal. We should and could talk more about this, especially since Vox in Spain and Chega in Portugal have made inroads into the politics of these two southern European countries. What one can observe is that the right-wing authoritarian regimes in these Western European countries had endured long enough to become weakened and at the same time for the opposition to grow in strength, so that the democracy that ensued saw both political poles, left and right, in some sort of balance in terms of economic power and presence in the civil society. On the other hand, it is interesting that even much longer (and probably much tougher) Communist regimes in the East allowed for some opposition to survive, but in such a fragile form that – when the changes came – there was absolutely no question of a power balance, except perhaps in the Czech Republic with its strong liberal and social democratic tradition and in Poland, where such a counterweight was enabled by the Catholic tradition.

But beyond the power ambitions of Mr Orbán or Mr Kaczyński, it would be essential to look beneath the surface of these governments' opposition to certain aspects of liberal democracy. The fact is that a lot of that opposition from the populist right has come as a result of the so-called 'cancel' culture, where dissent to some of the values, associated with liberal democracy, is not tolerated and not listened to – and not only in Eastern Europe. 'With some justification, it has been argued that the college campus – especially in the English-speaking world – is no longer reliably a gymnasium of the mind and has become, to a greater or lesser extent, a forcing house for various social justice causes that [...] threaten the core purpose of higher education as the rigorous transmission of truth, knowledge, expertise and the skills of dispassionate inquiry.'[203] In such an environment, far from being limited to academia, it can easily happen that a diverging opinion 'is so obnoxious that is not *like* violence but *actually* violence. You cannot speak unless I feel "safe" in every sense of the word. If I cannot actually censor you, I will seek to drive you out of the public space by "cancelling" you.' d'Ancona cites the notorious example of the cancelling campaign against J.K. Rowling which happened in the wider public arena.[204]

In addition to basic human rights and freedoms, multi-party democracy, and the checks and balances essential for a functioning democracy, European values now often seem to be reduced to what Chin called 'sexual democracy'. A proof of this seems to be President Macron's call in January 2022 for abortion to be added to the EU Charter of Fundamental Rights, apparently to counter the moves by the Polish government to narrow down the grounds for abortion. Equally problematic are the occasional statements or pieces of legislation in Poland and Hungary in relation to the LGBT+ community that many found discriminating or at least insulting.

As for abortion in Europe, it was by and large decriminalised and/or legalised against the backdrop of feminist demands that saw in abortion a way out from women's oppressive submission to male will and desperate social or health circumstances. In the absence of modern contraceptives, the right to abortion

---

203. d'Ancona, M, *Identity, Ignorance, Innovation: Why the Old Politics is Useless & What to Do About It*, Hodder & Stoughton, 2021, p. 24.
204. Ibid., p. 67.

was seen as personal, social and economic liberation. But a century later, with full female empowerment in the Western world, easy access to divorce, free pre- and post-natal care, paid maternity leave, economic and social emancipation of women and availability of (free of charge) contraceptives, these early twentieth-century grounds for abortion are not equally convincing. Nevertheless, despite these social changes, the right to abortion has been vigorously defended, and now comes to represent a sort of symbol of personal and bodily freedom and inviolability – a privacy issue. Such an approach has created a considerable obstacle to a more rational debate on the negative consequences of abortion on demand or on the very broad social grounds for it. We thus continue to see emotionally charged reactions to any suggestion to reduce the incidence of abortion (either by lowering the upper time limit, narrowing the grounds or by introducing social services aimed at reducing the demand for an abortion) or even attempts to discuss its ethical aspects. On the other hand, rushing through the chambers pieces of bills that dramatically restrict abortion rights, as done in Poland, is not helpful either, because it is seen – rightly or wrongly – as an imposition of the masculine conservative will over the freedom of women, all the more so under a socially conservative government.

Issues other than abortion are of even greater concern and fuel polarisation and populism. The same socially conservative stratum of society (in Eastern Europe and elsewhere) is also worried about what they perceive as a weakened European identity, Europe's failure to integrate migrants, in particular from Muslim countries, lack of interest in the persecution of Christians in the Middle East, about the marginalisation and vilifying of Christians in the West, as well as about efforts to codify gender theory and euthanasia. Many feel that we are witnessing a deliberate, ideologically driven campaign against traditional/Christian values, a true culture war being waged against what is now a Christian minority within European society. Little has been done to change that impression or to appease these fears or to enter into dialogue with them.

Within the geopolitical context, this culture war gets a further religious and international dimension, involving Catholics and Orthodox Christians. At least until the Russian invasion of Ukraine, there were many in Orthodox Eastern Europe and some among the more conservative Catholics in Central Europe that found Putin's call for a return to traditional values appealing. (Some continue to do so, despite the war in Ukraine.) Interestingly enough, even Pope Francis, whom many of the very same conservative Catholics would consider heretically progressive, agreed with Patriarch Kirill of Russia on a Joint Declaration in 2016, which among others expresses concern 'about the crisis in the family in many countries'. It declares that 'Orthodox and Catholics share the same conception of the family [...] based on marriage, an act of freely given and faithful love between a man and a woman' and regrets 'that other forms of cohabitation have been placed on the same level as this union'.[205] Apparently, for the sake of Christian unity and other pressing issues, Pope Francis agreed on a text that he had himself, in his own pastoral practice, in many ways already surpassed or at least complemented with a compassion and openness, unknown in the reasoning of the Russian Orthodox Church. In fact, within the first six years of Pope Francis's pontificate, President Putin visited the Vatican no less than three times – 'a privilege that the pope has not

---

205. https://mospat.ru/en/news/49758/ (Retrieved on 22.6.2022.)

given to any other international leader.'[206] This has certainly added to Putin's image as a *defensor fidei*,[207] whether intended or not.

There may be several reasons behind the pope's hospitality, e.g. his ecumenical efforts to bring the Churches closer and his view of the Orthodox Church as a rare ally on certain issues. After all, Pope Francis *is* a defender of family values, though understood in a broader context. However in a political sense, the pope's actions are at least in part seen as relativising the authoritarian nature of Putin; Matzuzzi concludes that 'Francis refuses a narrow choice between democracy and autocracy, between black and white',[208] although this is done out of his primary concern to save what can be saved, including with his new Eastern Politics versus China. This is intriguing given that Pope Francis has been also very critical of populism, saying that its various forms 'deform the meaning of the word "people" by hitching it to ideologies that focus on perceived enemies, internal and external'.[209] But reading the current pope is not easy, as he equally detests unfettered liberalism: 'If one worldview exalts and promotes the atomised individual, leaving little room for fraternity and solidarity, the other reduces the people to a faceless mass it claims to represent.'[210]

Pope Francis is thus walking a very narrow road in which (for pragmatic reasons) he is also willing to talk to the likes of Putin (or Patriarch Kirill of Moscow), but above all wants to

---

206. Matzuzzi, M, *Il Santo Realismo: Il Vaticano Come Potenza Politica Internazionale da Giovanni Paolo II a Francesco*, Luiss University Press, 2021, p. 106.
207. Ibid., p. 107.
208. Ibid., p. 126.
209. Pope Francis, *Let Us Dream: The Path to a Better Future*, Simon & Schuster, 2020, p. 107.
210. Ibid.

defend basic tenets of Christian faith and tradition, including strong emphasis on what are usually termed 'family values', now increasingly with a negative connotation in secular circles. At the same time he does not want to be seen in the camp of ultra-conservatives, as known from his widely publicised remarks on homosexuals – remarks seen by conservatives as an alarming attempt to change the teaching of the Church and as not going far enough by liberal Catholics. By the same token, the pope is not overly enthusiastic about pro-life campaigners (in the US), as long as some of them either defend or are untroubled by capital punishment and the unfettered freedom to bear arms.

This was clearly evident from the Vatican's official reaction to the June 2022 ruling of the U.S. Supreme Court on Roe v. Wade. Italian Archbishop Vincenzo Paglia, president of the Pontifical Academy for Life, said that 'the killing of an innocent human being can never be considered a "right". This goes for abortion, it goes for war, it goes for the death penalty and for the selling and use of arms'.[211] Similarly, the pope is not too impressed by the Polish Church or by Mr Orbán in his defence of Christian Europe. Obviously, social conservatism in Central Europe or in the United States is not something close to his heart: 'For example, a fantasy of national-populism in countries with Christian majorities is its defence of "Christian civilisation" from perceived enemies, whether Islam, Jews, the European Union, or the United Nations. [...]. irreligious or superficially religious people vote for populists to protect their religious identity, unconcerned that fear and

---

211. https://cruxnow.com/vatican/2022/06/vatican-official-says-roe-ruling-should-open-great-debate-on-protecting-life-at-every-stage (Retrieved on 26 July 2022.)

hatred of the other cannot be reconciled with the Gospel.'[212] But neither is he impressed by an increasingly individual society, in which personal freedom is turned 'into an ideology, creating a prism through which they judge everything'.[213] He is in fact concerned about 'the hyperinflation of the individual combined with weak institutions and the despotic control of the economy by a very few' and among those institutions 'the family has taken the hardest knock of all'.[214] In other words, he is no fan of the post-modern 'woke' agenda – he often speaks about all such ideologies as new forms of mental colonisation.

Concerns about European identity and guardianship of European values are not heard only in the Vatican. Philosopher and cultural theorist Kwame Anthony Appiah warns that 'values aren't a birthright: you need to keep caring about them. Living in the West, however you define it – being Western, however you define that – provides no guarantee that you will care about Western Civ'.[215] And he adds that 'what makes "us" a people, ultimately, is a commitment to governing a common life together',[216] and in another place: 'a nation is a group of people who think of themselves as sharing ancestry and also care about the fact that they have that supposed ancestry in common.'[217] This is very similar to what Scheffer wrote.

In another book, *Cynical Theories: How Activist Scholarship Made Everything About Race, Gender and Identity,* Helen Pluckrose and James Lindsay analyse in detail how the postmodernist philosophy of the 1960s developed a

---

212. Ibid., p. 119.
213. Ibid., p. 27.
214., Ibid. p. 46.
215. Appiah, KA, *The Lies That Bind: Rethinking Identity*, Profile Books 2018, p.211.
216. Ibid., p. 102.
217. Ibid., p. 76.

new ideology in the following decades – the theory of Social Justice (with capital letters), which prevailed in the twenty-first century in academic as well as in social discourse, especially in the field of gender issues.

Sometimes this mentality is inaccurately or superficially called liberal, but the authors – themselves advocates of liberal ideas – claim the opposite. They say that this new ideology is not about liberal tolerance and acceptance of homosexuals and various other life choices or ways of living, much less about promoting social, racial, and sexual equality. The authors show very convincingly that this dictatorship of political correctness is a far-left signature of complete opposition to classical liberalism, of imposing the only acceptable philosophical view that has grown into an ideology, almost into a religion.

This postmodernism is described by the authors as marked by radical scepticism about any possibility of objective cognition and at the same time by a commitment to cultural constructivism, and a belief that society is purely a system of power. Postmodernism, in the authors' view, blurs the boundaries, uses the language of power, and introduces cultural relativism and the loss of the individual and the universal.[218]

In the context of our discussion on sexual democracy, it is interesting to note Pluckrose's and Lindsay's criticism of the 'woke' for almost completely ignoring biology, as 'it regards the very existence of categories of sex, gender, and sexuality to be oppressive'.[219] In this area 'theory's political agenda is to challenge what is called *normativity* – that some things are more common or regular to the human condition, thus

---

218. Pluckrose, H, Lindsay, J, *Cynical Theories: How Activist Scholarship Made Everything about Race, Gender and Identity*, Pitchstone Publishing 2020, p. 31.
219. Ibid., p. 89.

more normative from a social (thus moral) perspective, than others. The main industry of queer theorists is to intentionally conflate two meanings of "normative", and deliberately make strategic use of the moral understanding of the term to contrive problems with its descriptive meaning.'[220] This way of thinking is engaged in 'ridiculing normative sexualities and genders and depicting those who recognise them as backwards and boorish. [...] Furthermore, the idea that heterosexuality is a social construct completely neglects the reality that humans are sexually reproducing species. The idea that homosexuality is a social construct neglects the plentiful evidence that it is also a biological reality.'[221]

But the authors emphasise that 'liberalism does not require one to believe that gender and sexuality are socially constructed in order to argue that there is no justification for discriminating against anyone'.[222] They point out that 'postmodern theory and liberalism do not merely exist in tension: they are almost directly at odds with one another. Liberalism sees knowledge as something we can learn about reality, more or less objectively'.[223] On the other side, 'illiberalism is easily recognisable in totalitarian, hierarchical, censorious, feudal, patriarchal, colonial, or theocratic states'.[224] However, 'it is opposed not to conservatism in general, but to the kind of conservatism that seeks to conserve hierarchies of class, race, or gender.'[225] This is contrary to critical race and related theories that use a 'simplistic identity politics approach which

---

220. Ibid., p. 94.
221. Ibid., pp. 109 – 110.
222. Ibid., p. 100.
223. Ibid., p. 237.
224. Ibid., p. 244.
225. Ibid., p. 245.

ascribes collective blame to dominant groups'.[226] Pluckrose and Lindsay (the latter was permanently suspended from Twitter in August 2022 for violating rules against hate speech), who at this point somehow naturally comes to mention Mr Orbán (as the person who promoted a ban on gender studies), insist that we cannot fight illiberalism with illiberalism, and at the same time warn that 'through the systematic and near-total silencing of reasonable and moderate voices from the left, center, and center-right, Social Justice opens itself and our society up most precariously and certainly to an authoritarian far-right backlash.'[227]

Is this what has been in fact happening in Poland and Hungary, but also elsewhere? It seems David Goodhart would at least partially agree. In addition to the 'trinity of populist concerns – immigration, security and corruption'[228] [of liberal elites], he devotes an entire chapter of his book *The Road to Somewhere* to the issues of family and gender. He argues that we have lost sight of 'how to create new forms of mutually beneficial inter-dependence between men and women in an era of equality between the sexes, and how to preserve the two-parent family, so far as possible, in an era of greater freedom'.[229] So it is not only about the abandoning of Christian family values, but also within the liberal camp there is concern about the departure from Humanistic philosophy.

Elsewhere, Rob Riemen, the well-known Dutch liberal thinker, offers an analysis of the relationship between the decline of Humanism and the rise of Fascism. He agrees that

---

226. Ibid., p. 262.
227. Ibid., p. 262.
228. Goodhart, D, *The Road to Somewhere: The Populist Revolt and the Future of Politics*, Hurst 2017, p. 57.
229. Ibid., p. 195.

today 'there is unmistakably a deep cultural crisis in our society. We no longer know what our common spiritual values are...'[230] Furthermore, 'our society is a kitsch society because it disregards the highest good, spiritual values, and we live our entire existence under the emblem of pleasure. [...] Because there are no longer any absolute spiritual values, there is no objective measure for our actions, and everything becomes subjective.'[231] But contrary to most social conservatives, he believes that 'a far greater threat to our society than Islamic fundamentalism is the crisis inherent in mass society: the moral crisis, the ever increasing trivialisation and dumbing-down of our society'. He rightly warns the advocates of Christian values that 'the defender of Judeo-Christian and humanistic traditions will always believe in a universal ethics that includes all people'[232] and strongly believes that the PVV party, mentioned earlier in relation to my Dutch experience, 'is the shameless opposite of the Judeo-Christian and humanist traditions'.[233] He would also have this to say to social conservatives and (Christian) fundamentalists in Eastern Europe and elsewhere: 'People are left high and dry by conservative intellectuals who simply cannot understand that precisely because truth is absolute, we always have to be prepared for the changing shapes of truth through different periods, and that to be faithful to truth and to live in truth, we have to look out for the new, for change.'[234] He warns against populism as the 'kitsch culture of the mass-man', which, if coupled with nationalism, turns into fascism.[235] But it

---

230. Riemen, R, *To Fight Against This Age: On Fascism and Humanism*, W. W. Norton & Company, 2018, p. 64.

231. Ibid., p. 73.

232. Ibid., p. 67.

233. Ibid., p. 68.

234. Ibid., p. 77.

235. Ibid., p. 80.

is, above all, 'the spiritual vacuum in which fascism can grow large again'[236] – something many Christians would certainly agree with.

As would, probably, Charles Taylor, Canadian philosopher and author of the famous book *A Secular Age,* 'the most important work about religion in our times',[237] who also expresses concerns about the departure of European civilisation from its Humanistic roots: 'Their denigration by modern humanism, in the name of equality, happiness and an end to suffering, was what was degrading the human being, reducing human life to something no longer worth living, spreading "nihilism". In our day, this attack against civilising humanism has been taken up by Michel Foucault. [...] This was the (not really explicit) ethical meaning behind the much trumpeted "end of man"; as it is the point of the denunciation of "humanism" among many post-modernists.'[238] In fact, Taylor believes that the current post-modern trends are not only secular and alien to religious understanding of the world, but also anti-humanist, putting the basic values of our (European or Western) civilisation under threat in a way that is difficult to withstand: 'And the farther one moves to a "post-modern", "anti-humanist" position, the more a passionate commitment to universal rights is without grounding in the nature of things, and without hope of reward or fulfilment, the more unmotivated in traditional terms this commitment is, as with Derrida for instance, then the more it is plainly powered by a sense of dignity, the sense of a demand laid on us by our very lucidity. This seems admirable and heroic. And

---

236. Ibid., p. 85.
237. Halík, T, *I Want You to Be: On the God of Love*, University of Notre Dame Press, 2016, p. 55.
238. Taylor, p. 635.

in a way undoubtedly is. But a question arises of whether it is an adequate source, that is, whether it can really motivate us to carry through on our aspiration to universal human dignity and well-being.'[239] He is concerned about what he terms as 'exclusive humanism' (by which he means a humanism devoid of any transcendence), because this new type of humanism demands that 'you can't be fully into contemporary humanist concerns if you haven't sloughed off the old beliefs. You can't be fully with the modern age and still believe in God'.[240]

But he too is not convinced by those that 'look back and see the glorious past of Christendom, be it in the European Middle Ages, or in the early modern period, or in the time before the French Revolution, or before the Reformation; or even, as with the American "Christian Right", the age they want to restore is only a few decades in the past'.[241] What he calls for is another type of Christianity that is not hostile to liberalism at all – but also rejects the 'secular fundamentalism' of what he calls 'polite society', antagonistic to Christianity.

The same issue occupies the mind of the Czech philosopher and Templeton Prize recipient Tomáš Halík. He rejects both the 'naively militant "new atheism" of Richard Dawkins and Co. and, on the other hand, its equally noisy and similarly naïve counterparts: Christian fundamentalism and the "religious Right"'.[242] Instead, in his view, the future of our Western civilisation 'depends on the capacity of two types of humanism to coexist and be mutually compatible, namely Christian humanism and secular humanism'.[243] This is because

---

239. Taylor, p. 695.
240. Ibid., p. 572.
241. Ibid., p. 733.
242. Halík, p. 61.
243. Ibid., p. 149.

'were Christianity to turn its back on modernity it would sink into bigotry and fundamentalist religion, and conversely, were modernity to turn away completely from Christianity it would itself become an intolerant pseudo-religion'.[244] (Is this what is happening in, for example, Poland and with the Christian Right in the United States?) Therefore, 'the decisive battle about the complexion of our civilisation – particularly a unifying Europe – will most likely take place *within liberalism itself*, between two models of liberalism [...] namely, between the *pluralist model*, which seeks to create space for mutual respect and freedom for all (including in respect of religion), and the *universalist model*, which presents liberalism as a binding ideology.'[245] It is a battle that we, however, still yearn to see.

In any event, these examples explain some of the genuine concerns at the root of different types of populisms across Europe and Central Europe in particular. There, issues of migration, security, identity, governance, the economy, the urban-rural divide and also 'sexual democracy' have had their distinct imprint, characterised by the region's social history. As we saw in the first part of this book, Enlightenment ideas arrived with some delay in Central Europe, and the Austro-Hungarian Empire also kept the ideals of the French Revolution at bay. Its economic development was equally not generally conducive to a more liberal society. Finally, the Iron Curtain allowed for only limited spread of post-war philosophical and social trends in Europe, which also helped preserve social conservatism, seen in those times also as a silent opposition to the Communist system. Few classically liberal pockets of resistance survived, with some exceptions in the Czech

---

244. Ibid., p. 150.
245. Ibid., p. 154, italics are author's.

Republic (with its liberal and industrial pre-war traditions) and in a couple of other large urban centres.

Moreover, the Communist regimes built a dense social network connecting businesses, administration, media and arts, which – with some difference from country to country – has to a large extent weathered the democratic changes in 1990s and can now be seen as a serious obstacle to economic and media pluralism, and to liberal democracy in general. In parallel, attempts to introduce liberal and in particular post-modern ideas after the democratic changes and Eastern Europe's return to Europe have not always gone down well in the region, especially when the agents of these ideological currents were seen as associated either with the remnants of the 'old guard' or with the nascent new elite or with copying of the West, as Holmes and Krastev suggested. As a result we have seen in Eastern Europe the rise of fundamentalist conservative and Christian ideology in a stronger fashion than in the West, where another type of fundamentalism seems to reign – the postmodern, a universalist form of an aggressive secular liberalism.

For all these reasons, populism and backsliding of the rule of law in Central Europe should all give us pause for thought – and should also trouble those in the West, equally plagued by different types of populism, xenophobia and even perhaps of trends that could result in the return of Fascism, as Rob Riemen warns us. Recipes on how to fight back should be specific and should not be seen as ideologically driven by post-modern 'woke', which many see as a contemporary version of the Communist threat of pre-war Europe: there are many Christians and other conservatives out there that are scared at the prospect of a new woke totalitarianism that will restrict religious freedom, impinge on the concept of objection of conscience and effectively push them out of the public sphere, making them a second class citizen. But true liberal democracy should not, in principle, have a problem with (socially) conservative policies or religion, Christianity included. Moreover, secularism that does not recognise the potential of religion for social dialogue (and also for the integration of immigrants) will not help. By the same token, social conservatism that does not reject classic liberal freedoms and the European Humanist tradition should be respected, otherwise the defenders of liberal democracy and the rule of law risk alienating important sections of population, East and West. In fact, we need – as Halík has stressed – a coalition of liberals and conservatives, left and right, forging an agreement on an inclusive set of European values that would – while respecting the secular and diverse character of European society today – give recognition to the Christian and Humanist traditions as central pillars of European identity. At the same time, without looking deeper at the roots of left or right populism and other challenges to the rule of law – while not giving in to autocrats – there is a risk of creating new divisions, helping replicate conditions that Europe faced in the 1930s, and deepening the gap between the two halves of Europe at this critical time in its history.

Epilogue:
The Future of Eastern Europe

In 1945, Communism forced Ljubo, Karl and many other Eastern European political emigrés to seek shelter in Western Europe. At that time, these refugees did not realise they were leaving behind 'Eastern Europe'. There was no such thing then. They felt that – after the nightmare of Nazi and Fascist terror – their own countries had been overtaken by another alien ideology that was so opposed to everything they knew from before that life became unbearable. These were Karl's words exactly: he could not stand the Communist regime's uniformity, which was so alien to him. This new ideology was (literally) after their lives – Ljubo was sentenced to death, a fate he only narrowly escaped. Many others who stayed at home felt much the same, if not perhaps so intensely. There were also so many that did not have the means, the opportunity or simply the courage to leave, but few of them were comfortable with the new system. It was certainly not something that they, by the mere fact of being Eastern Europeans, could put up with. One can hardly compare the sense of frustration and desperation of those that left and of those that stayed on.

Where is Eastern Europe today? What do we know about it? Low-cost airlines have done part of the job. Many (young) people have since visited the region, which is now much more familiar to them than even a decade ago. But has Eastern

Europe indeed become a normal place? And what about populism and social conservatism there, of which we can read almost daily? Are these inherent features of this part of Europe? Is there, after all, indeed something *Eastern* about Eastern Europe, as the first edition of this book was asking? Is Eastern Europe indeed the cradle of the so-called illiberal Europe, as analysed in this new edition?

With the help of the EU Single Market, EU funds, and despite the drain of many young people, the region has weathered the multiple crises of the last two decades with surprising resilience. The goals for which they fought for so long – membership in the EU and NATO, the Eurozone and Schengen – have been achieved and are now seen as a means to an end, rather than as goals. Over almost two decades of EU membership, Central Europe has grown into an assertive, economically viable and prosperous, politically fairly stable and efficient part of the EU. It is also a fast growing market for the Western member states, a source of a relatively cheap and qualified workforce, as well as considerable capital gains from foreign investments.

More and more, this part of Europe is now also making its own contribution to the foreign and security policies of Europe – even if the region's approach to Russia was, until the Russian invasion of Ukraine, not appreciated in the West and its sensitivities and fears perceived in Brussels as overblown. 'Here Slovenia was a step ahead of us,' a Finnish diplomat wrote to me in response to my congratulations on Finland's decision to enter NATO in the spring of 2022.

Indeed, under Polish-Baltic leadership, NATO has decided to strengthen its eastern flank, as the war in Ukraine has helped to bring Central Europe more to the centre of the attention of the international community and the West in particular, including again the United States. The case of Ukraine may even affect the whole concept of EU enlargement. We will probably see more geopolitics discussed in relation to Ukraine and Moldova (a country too often forgotten), as well as with the Western Balkans.

More mixed is, as this book acknowledges, the region's record on the political and governance side. Ruling parties in Poland and Hungary have now for years been accused of capturing the state with a socially conservative, populist or outright illiberal and fundamentalist ideology. Even in the otherwise traditionally liberal and pro-Western Czech Republic, both current President Zeman (his term expires in 2023) and former Prime Minister and magnate Babiš (in office from 2017 to 2021) have been blamed for populist tendencies. In neighbouring Slovakia, the political and judicial system was shaken to the core by the murder of an investigative journalist Ján Kuciak in 2018 and by the struggle of the system to bring the killers (and those that ordered the execution) to justice. In Slovenia, three consecutive elections (2014, 2018 and 2022) propelled to the post of Prime Minister political novices, so-called new faces. There, as in some other instances, the capture of the state and populism is believed to have a different ideological character. To add to this are the region's controversial reaction to the migrant crisis of 2015/2016 and the reluctance of some of the countries to embrace certain aspects of the so-called LGBT+ agenda, understood now as an essential part of the new generation of human rights.

Does all this mean that a distinct version of Europe, an illiberal Europe, is indeed emerging in Central and Eastern Europe? A political and geographic phenomenon akin to the illiberal drive in Western Europe, that some, for example Rob Riemen, see as a precursor to (new) fascism, which he defines as a cocktail of the kitsch culture of the mass-man, a large dose of nationalism, resentment and hatred?[246] In Eastern Europe, which disproportionally suffered from twentieth-century Fascism and Nazism, that assessment seems somewhat preposterous, though in some countries of the region extreme right wing movements do exist – surely as an absurd caricature, given the crimes committed by Nazis and Fascists in their countries. In any event, the political developments described are problematic, and the populist or fundamentalist ideology of some of the governments does pose questions about the future of liberal democracy in Central and Eastern Europe.

'Western liberalism is still skating on thin ice' too, despite the 'shot in the arm' by Mr Putin and his invasion of Ukraine, writes Edward Luce.[247] It could be further endangered (and Ukraine negatively affected) by Trump's eventual return to the White House. Eyebrows have also been raised in Italy with the election of the Meloni government. Interesting to note was the link that some liberal observers made between the new Italian government and populism in Eastern Europe: 'Meloni is too close to Hungary and Poland...'[248] But Timothy Garton Ash confidently concludes that for a fascist revival one should look to Moscow (not Rome),[249] where the cult of a macho leader, cultivation of historical resentment, state-sponsored doctrine and demonisation of the enemy make a toxic cocktail, now seen at work in Ukraine.

With the 2022 Russian invasion of Ukraine, it is far from

---

246. Riemen, p. 80.
247. 'Western liberalism is still skating on thin ice', *Financial Times*, 28 September 2022.
248. 'Italy at risk of turning back on Brussels in favour of east Europe, tycoon warns', *Financial Times*, 21 September 2022.
249. 'For a fascist revival look to Moscow, not Rome', *Financial Times*, 30 September 2022.

certain which course the politics of Central and Eastern Europe (and also its image) will take in an equally uncertain future. The region's reaction to the 2015 migration wave has been largely forgotten thanks to the Polish welcome of 3.5 million Ukrainian refugees. (Czechs, Baltics and others followed suit with unprecedented assistance.) But did this amount to an atonement for the region's stance in the 2015/2016 migration crisis? To say the least, the cultural aspect of this reaction remains unresolved. The same goes for the new EU asylum policy. (The UK after Brexit does not find it any easier either – think of the Rwanda plan and illegal crossings of the Channel). And we have not even touched upon how the international community should address migration issues on the global scale. The so-called Global Compact on Migration, agreed at UN level in 2016, solves little.

In the Central European tier of Eastern Europe, which is already for some time a part of the European Union, the political debate in the future will surely centre around foreign policy, energy mix, response to climate change, and access to and aims of EU funds, but also about fundamentals, like European values, including, of course, the rule of law. This discussion is essential, though it is not an exercise solely needed in the Eastern part of the continent.

The op-ed by Mateusz Morawiecki, the Polish Prime Minister from August 2022,[250] six months into the war in Ukraine, provides an interesting example of such discussion. The Polish leader takes the ongoing war in Ukraine as his point of departure, saying that it 'has exposed the truth about Russia' and about the 'imperialist tendencies' of Putin's state, but also the truth about Europe, whose many leaders

---

250. https://www.reuters.com/world/europe/polish-pm-calls-reform-against-eu-imperialism-welt-op-ed-2022-08-10/

'allowed themselves to be lured by Vladimir Putin'. However, in the Polish Prime Minister's confident view, this is not because Europe 'was insufficiently integrated, but because it refused to listen to the voice [...] coming from Poland' which is 'in matters of relations with Russia [...] simply far more experienced than others'. He continues that this ignorance of Poland is just an example of the broader problem of the equality of individual countries in the EU: 'Political practice has shown that the voice of Germany and France counts above all. [...] In addition, the strong ones make mistakes and are incapable of accepting criticism from outside.' He advocates for preservation of the principle of unanimity in the EU, and to make the case against abolishing this principle he – probably rather unfortunately from the point of view of Berlin – gives the example of Germany, saying that '[i]f all of Europe would have followed Germany's voice, not only Nord Stream 1, but also Nord Stream 2 would have been launched for many months'. Furthermore and returning to the argument of migration, had this principle been abandoned '[w]e would be an object rather than a subject of international politics today if the European Union, instead of a tough policy of defending its own borders – a fundamental attribute of state sovereignty – had also adopted the rules for distribution of migrants proposed in 2015. Back then, Putin noticed that migrants could be used as a tool in a hybrid war against the EU [...] Our resilience to the next big crisis would be even lower today if we had listened to open borders advocates in 2015'. He then goes even further in his lambasting of Germany with the following words: 'if all of Europe would have sent weapons to Ukraine on the same scale and at the same pace that Germany does – the war would have ended long ago. It would have ended with Russia's absolute victory. And Europe would be on the eve of another war.' (Relations with Germany received another blow a couple of months later, when Polish government sent to Berlin a formal request for World War II reparations valued at 1.3 trillion EUR.)

Morawiecki then turns to EU values, repeating the argument about freedom and equality, but applying this to financial matters, targeting Germany yet again, which traditionally held a positive balance of foreign trade: 'The adoption of a common currency does not guarantee sustainable and harmonious development. In fact, the euro introduces mechanisms of mutual rivalry, which can be seen, for example, in the permanent export surplus of some countries, which counteract the appreciation of their own currency by maintaining economic stagnation in others. In such a system, equal opportunities remain only on paper.' In his eyes, '[t]hese deficits make the European Union particularly vulnerable and weak when confronted with Russian imperialism'.

And although Poland is one of the biggest EU member states, the Polish Prime Minister tries to appeal to smaller member states by saying that in the EU of today 'the rights, interests or needs of medium-sized and small states are losing out when confronted with the largest states' and 'European solidarity is becoming an empty concept'. Other Central European countries may agree on this, though they would not necessarily subscribe to all that the Polish Prime Minister had to say.

In short, 'the European Union order does not protect us enough from external imperialism. The EU's institution and actions, while not being free from the temptation to dominate the weaker, remain exposed to the infiltration of Russian imperialism.' So the EU must first help Ukraine in her struggle, but it 'must also defeat the threat of imperialism within the

EU. We need a profound reform that would bring back the common good and equality to the top of the EU's principles.'

And here he touches upon the (future) architecture of the Union, where we need a 'change of optics – it is the member-states, and not the EU institutions, that must decide about the directions and priorities of the EU's actions, since it is the institutions that are created for the states, and not the other way around. [...] The problem, however, is not that we walk our path to integration too slowly and should rapidly accelerate this process.'

This has for some time been the position of Poland and to a large extent the entire Višegrad Four. But the Polish Prime Minister is less explicit on how the European common good can be secured via a different path and only vaguely speaks about 'returning to the principles underlying the European Union', rather than 'strengthening the institutional superstructure'. So he does not explain how exactly the EU, with a lesser supranational structure, can actively work against Russian ambitions. Interestingly, he also does not develop further the reference to the principles and values.

So the challenge of the so-called 'illiberal Europe' (despite some gestures of goodwill on the side of Warsaw) in the region remains, perhaps above all in Hungary. There some concessions have been made to Brussels' demands with regard to the rule of law, but the country failed to fit fully into the frame of the European response to the war in Ukraine. Hungary is also taking a much more lenient approach to China, which some would see as compatible with the alleged authoritarian tendencies in Hungary (and others as plain pragmatism). At the same time, the Polish attitude to Russia and China is exactly the opposite. There is also no sympathy for the Russian traditionalist narrative, despite the strength of Polish Catholicism. In fact, in a July 2022 meeting, the Polish and Hungarian Prime Ministers publicly acknowledged their differences.

Whatever we may think of illiberal tendencies in Eastern Europe – and we should certainly be worried about them – they do raise issues about what the root causes of such attitudes are. After all, similar underlying reasons for the rise of populism exist in Western Europe. But nowhere can populism, fundamentalism or worse be won over by a judgemental approach, cancelling out dissenting opinions, and by denying conservative views due legitimacy. One of the possible ways to confront social conservatism in its extreme forms (both East and West) should be by redressing the grievances heard by their representatives and voters. And these are and will continue to be many, according to Charles Dumas, 'from job displacement by hi-tech, from E[uro]A[rea] imbalances, from inequality of income and wealth, from structural weakness and continued debt escalation in Japan, in diffuse fashion from effects of the emergence of China as a power equal to the US, and arguably from malignant manipulation of populist dissent by a decadent and declining Russia'. To all these Dumas proposes solutions that do not sound politically viable at this time, such as EU fiscal Union or letting Greece and Italy leave the Eurozone.[251] The latter especially would bring political havoc to Europe.

But overall, much more than economy and politics as usual is needed. In fact, and as suggested by Tomáš Halík, Rob Riemen and others, we need to look at the basics, return to Europe's moral underpinning. To secure a future for the global West and for Europe at their best, we need a coalition of classic liberal Humanism and Judeo-Christian tradition, the two main pillars of European identity and values.

---

251. Dumas, C, *Populism and Economics*, Profile Books, 2018, pp. 156 – 158.

Religions could, contrary to prevailing attitudes, play an important role in this exercise. There is indeed 'a growing appreciation that mobilising communities in support of social objectives is often much easier when public authorities and religious communities work together'.[252] In order to do that 'we need a richer understanding of the terms "religion", "secular", and "the public sphere". Religious communities should act responsibly, acknowledging that political, social, and juridical arrangements are amenable to reason and debate. Public authorities should understand and recognise the different standpoints and responsibilities of religious communities'.[253] More generally, 'serious politics means giving due weight to the realm of religion and human values'.[254] The authors of the book, whose main argument is for an increased role of religion in international affairs 'argue for a new sensitivity – a "post-secular sensitivity" – to the role that religion can play in enlarging our understanding of the most pressing challenges of our time and unifying our efforts in response'.[255]

This liberal and conservative coalition should steer clear from both excessive social conservatism and fundamentalism (and certainly from any flirting with modern manifestations of Fascism), as well as from post-modern extreme political correctness and aggressive secularism (and nostalgia for Communism in some places) – the latter is also prone to totalitarian tendencies. George Orwell's *1984* equally resembles a right-wing, a Communist or a 'woke' dictatorship. Should Europe and the West choose one of these totalitarian

---

252. McDonagh, P, et al, *On the Significance of Religion for Global Diplomacy*, Routledge, 2021, p. 12.
253. Ibid., p. 14.
254. Ibid., p. 71.
255. Ibid., p. 134.

options there will, unlike in the post-World War II period, be nowhere to flee for these modern political refugees. For them, there is no such West anymore.

What we need instead is a complete reinvention of the political mainstream. We are in dire need of moderate politicians with firm values and clear vision, left and right, conservative, liberal and social democratic, East and West. Of those that Rachman sees as warriors in the 'struggle against the strongmen', Merkel and Macron, one is gone and the other, although re-elected, faces a difficult political situation at home.[256] Others praised as leaders of the liberal West of today have a relatively easy job to dismiss verbally often clumsy conservative authoritarian leaders, but they will need more than just a trendy public appeal and cool images, which tend to bend towards the post-modern and are obviously not inclusive enough. What is needed, is a return to the fundamentals of the West, though not in a fundamentalist way. This is very much a must for conservative governments in Eastern Europe too. It is certainly not tenable to 'put a reasonable face on rightwing populism' to get elected, as Steve Bannon is believed to have advised Giorgia Meloni.[257] Their distinct set of values must be rooted in compassion and inclusion, a face of free and open mind. By the same token, rising rightwing populism cannot be an excuse for a witchhunt. A new social contract must patiently and undoubtedly painstakingly be built in a very inclusive way for our liberal democracies to survive.

For the present mood might change and society get tired of uncertain subjectivism and of the loneliness of radical individualism, which could otherwise also start harming the

---

256. Rachman, p. 187.
257. 'Western liberalism is skating on thin ice', *Financial Times*, 28 September 2022.

social cohesion essential for a welfare state. But ideological fundamentalism, lack of compassion towards minority groups of all kinds, and new nationalisms will also not address the negative aspects of this globalised world.

As far as the specifics of Eastern Europe are concerned, I have been trying to show how its different history has affected the development of populisms in the region – both before and after World War II and the imposition of the Communist system. The region is unique to the extent that in the twentieth century it experienced all three European totalitarian systems, of which Communism is its latest experience – to many of the people of the region also the dominant one. Combined with the historically late arrival of the Enlightenment and, above all, with relative isolation from social and philosophical developments in post-war Western Europe, this resulted in a specific legacy. The latter has allowed for the preservation of a socially conservative mindset, as well as – at least in some places – the continued dominance of informal centres of power in the institutions of the state and in the civil society. The end result is a polarised society, with frustrated segments of the population, and a poor record of the state in relation to the rule of law, which could pave the way to an authoritarian future. This is especially dangerous when faced with crisis situations like those experienced in the recent past (financial, migration and health) or present (the war in Ukraine, energy and food security issues, as well as the return of migrants). This requires much more than the annual exercise of the EU Rule of Law Reports, especially since these papers do not get beneath the normative surface. In fact, no serious attempt to tackle the deficiencies to the rule of law in Eastern Europe can avoid addressing or at least acknowledging and taking into account the region's totalitarian past and its consequences.

This book has also been arguing that – while strongly rejecting views that are in opposition with the basic tenets of liberal democracy – the roots of populism in Europe have something to do with the question of what exactly liberal democracy and above all the European identity are and what European values actually are. The conference on the future of Europe and the emergence of the European Commission's portfolio on the European way of life attest that this is far more than an academic question – even if, or all the more, because neither of them seem to have produced tangible results. In that respect, developments in Central and Eastern Europe as described have a significance and pose questions that are relevant far beyond the region. One certainly cannot be content with the current Polish and Hungarian answer to these questions (little else has come from other countries in the region, so perhaps there is some untapped potential), but neither has the West nor Europe as a whole produced a real answer – yet. We are rather seeing a helpless convergence of social-democrats, liberals and people's parties around a loose, ill-defined and colour-less set of values and rights, blind about historic and cultural context. But such often aggressive post-modern secularism that in one stroke excludes conservative sections of the society is not a viable answer neither.

In fact, it seems that we are more distant from answers to the questions about European values than we were in the early post-war period, when the foundations of the European institutions (Council of Europe and the EU) were laid. Unfortunately, we also seem to be much further away from those answers than we were at the time of the fall of the Berlin Wall. We must therefore reflect well on the past 30 years, East and West, and act upon these reflections. European values as now enshrined in the EU treaties should be expressed in a much clearer way, a more inclusive list of values should not shy away from Europe's classic bedrock, and these values should be internalised by society and political leaders. Jan Zobec, a judge of the Slovenian Supreme Court and to some a black sheep of Slovenian judiciary explains: 'If a critical mass of people does not internalise the values of constitutionality, does not respect the law, does not take it seriously, if people are not integrated normatively, then even good functioning of the courts will not suffice. Constitutional and democratic culture is a long process. [...] Several generations are required, also the support of international environment and determination of key stakeholders in society, that is to say those that hold societal and political power... [...] It is about three pillars of the construction of social habitus: family, educational system and media. This is why key cultural battles are being fought in these fields...'[258] To that end we need a much more inclusive debate (including in the aforementioned two organisations), again both East and West, taking into account the different traditions and historical experiences that together have made and continue to make Europe.

---

258. *Demokracija* weekly, issue 38, year XXVII, 22 September 2022.

Bibliography

Throughout this book there are numerous references to a variety of literature I have used. Here I only list those sources that have been extensively used in the writing or which I consider particularly relevant, or those that I have found especially inspiring.

For a detailed account of the Christianisation of Europe, including Central Europe, see Richard Fletcher, *The Barbarian Conversion: From Paganism to Christianity* (New York, 1997). The last days of the (Western) Roman Empire are examined in Bryan Ward-Perkins, *The Fall of Rome and the End of Civilisation* (Oxford, 2005), which also gives an interesting explanation of why the Western Empire disappeared, while the Eastern one carried on. An equally fascinating account of the Byzantine Empire can be found in Warren Treadgold, *A Concise History of Byzantium* (Palgrave, 2001) or in Averil Cameron, *The Byzantines* (Blackwell, 2009), which I particularly recommend. In his highly readable *Byzantine Christianity: Emperor, Church and the West* (Detroit, 1982) Harry J Magoulias deals with the religious aspects of Byzantine Christianity and its relationship with the West. *The Myth of Nations: The Medieval Origins of Europe* (Princeton, 2002) is a very provocative reading of the myths about the early formation of the European nations, written by

241

Patrick J Geary. It leaves all kinds of nationalism, both big and small, looking a bit silly. The general idea of Europe is studied from a number of perspectives in *The Idea of Europe: From Antiquity to the European Union* (Woodrow Wilson Centre, 2002), edited by Anthony Pagden, as well as in Robert Bartlett, *The Making of Europe: Conquest, Colonisation and Cultural Change 950–1350* (Penguin, 1994). A brilliant book on the subject of Europe is Michael Heffernan's *The Meaning of Europe: Geography and Geopolitics* (Arnold, 1998), where the geographic aspect is particularly strong and fascinating. JHH Weiler defends Europe's Christian roots in *Un' Europa Cristiana* (BUR saggi, 2003).

Maria Todorova's *Imagining the Balkans* (Oxford University Press, 1997) is a rather academic, but very thorough and well-argued critical account of stereotypes about the Balkans. The interaction between Islam and Europe is the subject of another book by Richard Fletcher, *The Cross and the Crescent: Christianity and Islam from Muhammad to the Reformation* (Penguin, 2003).

Paula Sutter Fichtner complements a historical account of the Austrian Empire with social and cultural comments in *The Habsburg Monarchy, 1490–1848* (Palgrave Macmillan, 2003). The emergence of Germany is described in Harold James, *A German Identity* (London, 2000). Friedrich Naumann's *Central Europe* (New York, 1917) is now of great historic curiosity only. The post-World War I years are brilliantly described in Margaret MacMillan's highly readable *Peacemakers: The Paris Conference of 1919 and Its Attempt to End War* (London, 2001), which is of great help in understanding why Europe went to war once again in 1939. A similarly excellent account of the civilisation of the entire continent is Eric von Kuehnelt-Leddihn's *The Intelligent American's Guide to*

Europe (Arlington House, 1979), also a must-read for every intelligent European trying to understand European history, even nearly 50 years after its publication. It is probably the best book I have ever read about European civilisation. More conventional, but still very readable, is JM Roberts's *History of Europe* (Penguin, 1997).

My main source for the general history of Central Europe (although limited to the history of the Czech lands, Slovakia, Poland and Hungary) was Piotr S Wandycz, *The Price of Freedom, A History of East Central Europe from the Middle Ages to the Present* (Routledge, 2001). *The Palgrave Concise Historical Atlas of Eastern Europe* (Palgrave, 2001) by Dennis P Hupchick and Harold E Cox was an excellent companion. Adrian Hyde-Price's *The International Politics of East Central Europe* (Manchester University Press, 1996) has a very valuable overview of bilateral relations in the region. Most of the economic data and observations in this book are based on *The Origins of Backwardness in Eastern Europe* (University of California Press, 1991) by Daniel Chirot (ed.), and Angus Maddison's *The World Economy: Historical Statistics* (OECD 2003). The latter presents the backbone of the economic arguments in my book, while the social and cultural aspects are in great part based on *Inventing Eastern Europe* (Stanford University Press, 1994) by Larry Wolff, which is a detailed study of the emergence of the concept of Eastern Europe, also with examples from literature.

A very good source of documents about the Cold War period is Martin McCauley's excellent *The Origins of the Cold War 1941–1949* (Pearson Longman, 2003). Events since the 1970s are the subject of Bülent Gökay's *Eastern Europe since 1970* (Pearson Longman, 2001). The modern geopolitical challenges in Eastern Europe are the subject of Ola Tunander et al (ed.), *Geopolitics in Post-wall Europe: Security, Territory and Identity* (PRIO, Sage, 1997) and Andrew H. Dawson and Rick Fawn (eds.), *The Changing Geopolitics of Eastern Europe* (Frank Cass, 2002). On the Baltics, I have made several references to Aliide Naylor's *The Shadow in the East: Vladimir Putin and the New Baltic Front* (IB Tauris, 2020).

Further on, Tony Judt's *Postwar* (William Heinemann: London, 2005) is not only an excellent social, political and cultural history of Europe, but also pays a great deal of attention to the developments in Eastern Europe, as does Norman Davies's *Europe East & West* (Jonathan Cape, London, 2006), which deals with the historical aspects of this book in more detail.

The revised edition of the book made use of a number of more recent books on some of the special topics. Let me mention at least some of them. (Others are referenced in footnotes.) The main references on the state of democracy in the region have been Wojciech Sadurski, *Poland's Constitutional Breakdown* (Oxford University Press, 2019), Paul Lendvai's *Europe's New Strongman*, (Oxford University Press, 2017) and a book by the Slovenian legal scholars Matej Avbelj and Jernej Letnar Černič', *The Impact of European Institutions on the Rule of Law and Democracy: Slovenia and Beyond* (Hart Publishing, 2020). The economic aspect of developments in Central Europe is well explored and explained in Dorothee Bohle's and Béla Greskovits's *Capitalist Diversity on Europe's Periphery* (Cornell University Press, 2012).

The liberal backslide in wider context is explored by Ivan Krastev's and Stephen Holmes's *The Light that Failed: A Reckoning* (Allen Lane, 2019), *After Europe* (University of Pennsylvania Press, 2017), also by Krastev, as well as Gideon Rachman's *The Age of the Strongman* (Bodley Head, London,

2022) and Rob Riemen's *To Fight Against This Age: On Fascism and Humanism* (W.W. Norton & Comnpany, 2018).

On migration, I wish to recommend three books in particular. The first is Paul Scheffer's seminal *Immigrant Nation* (Polity Press, 2011). More recent, written in the immediate aftermath of the 2015-2016 migration crisis, is *Refuge: Transforming a Broken Refugee System* by Alexander Betts and Paul Collier (Penguin Books, 2018). Integration issues and multiculturalism are researched in depth by Rita Chin in *The Crisis of Multiculturalism in Europe: A History* (Princeton University Press, 2017).

Three other books look critically at the contempt for contemporary populism and try to see what is beneath. David Goodhart's *The Road to Somewhere: The Populist Revolt and the Future of Politics* (Hurst & Company, London, 2017) offers a perspective that goes beyond political correctness, but stays clear of populism and xenophobia. Kwame A. Appiah's *The Lies that Bind: Rethinking Identity* (Profile Books, 2018) points out the continued need for identities, understood in a much more inclusive and complex way. More revisionist is Helen Pluckrose and James Lindsay's *Cynical Theories: How Activist Scholarship Made Everything about Race, Gender, and Identity – and Why This Harms Everybody* (Pitchstone Publishing, Durham, North Carolina, 2020) which advocates for a return to classic liberal values against postmodern ones.

Acknowledgements

First of all, my thanks go to Ion Mills at Oldcastle Books for the idea of a revised edition of my 2009 book on Eastern Europe.

Over the course of more than a decade, a number of readers of *What's So Eastern About Eastern Europe* have helped shape the thinking behind the revised edition with their comments. For new insights, I am also indebted to several authors of books about the state of mind of Europe and the world, most of which appear in the bibliography section and in the footnotes. I was fortunate enough to meet some of them.

I am particularly grateful to Prof Tomáš Halík, Rob Riemen. Enda O'Doherty and Prof Matej Avbelj for their time to read the manuscript and, of course, for their kind words on the text.

My thanks go to the team at Oldcastle Books: Nick Rennison as editor, Hollie McDevitt and Sarah Stewart-Smith in publicity and marketing, Steven Mair as proofreader and Ellie Lavender as publishing controller, who co-ordinated us all.

Last but not least, I am grateful to my wife Barbara for being my most faithful supporter with this book too.

Index

⊙LDCASTLE BOOKS

POSSIBLY THE UK'S SMALLEST
INDEPENDENT PUBLISHING GROUP

Oldcastle Books is an independent publishing company formed in 1985 dedicated to providing an eclectic range of titles with a nod to the popular culture of the day.

Imprints vary from the award winning crime fiction list, NO EXIT PRESS, to lists about the film industry, KAMERA BOOKS & CREATIVE ESSENTIALS. We have dabbled in the classics, with PULP! THE CLASSICS, taken a punt on gambling books with HIGH STAKES, provided in-depth overviews with POCKET ESSENTIALS and covered a wide range in the eponymous OLDCASTLE BOOKS list. Most recently we have welcomed two new digital first sister imprints with THE CRIME & MYSTERY CLUB and VERVE, home to great, original, page-turning fiction.

oldcastlebooks.com

OLDCASTLE BOOKS	KAMERA BOOKS	HIGHSTAKES PUBLISHING
POCKET ESSENTIALS	CREATIVE ESSENTIALS	THE CRIME & MYSTERY CLUB
NO EXIT PRESS	PULP! THE CLASSICS	VERVE BOOKS